CU00842017

1

First published 2018 by Zack Davies
Text and images © Zack Davies 2018

ISBN 978-1722127114

The Shadow Cabinet

POEMS 2016-2018

ZACK DAVIES

Table of Contents

Introduction

It is now three years since I first started wondering "Why not publish a book?", and, in that time period, I have found some pretty compelling reasons why not. Book 1 was an unnecessarily large doorstop with low quality control. My ego being what it is, I have felt compelled to put together another unnecessarily large doorstop of a book, with what I imagine to be better quality control. This will hopefully mean I do not have to put out any more massive tomes and can instead write dainty Faberesque pamphlets about foxgloves and wagtails.

Progress has been slow on Book 2, or rather the constituent parts of what became this book. This is mainly because I have been unable to stay awake on my morning train in, the window of opportunity within which most of Book 1 was written.

As ever, I thank the open mic hosts of Medway and my tolerant family.

Zack Davies, Kent, 2018

As I Was Saying Before I Was So Rudely Interrupted By My Own Indolence

The same ashamed obsessions
The listed glib concerns
The infinite regressions
Of he who never learns.
The roundabouts and cul-de-sacs,
The overstated haste;
The repetitions, crass and lax,
The lack of better taste.
My scripts insist I photostat
Or elsewise reproduce
What Xerox, yesterday, begat,
Then put it to said use.

Contemplate, cogitate, write and redraft,
Venting inventions of wrath
I punched out my lines but then nobody laughed
Until I got piss-bottled off
Plying my styles down at half-open mics
At venues in states of despair
The chump front of stage free to do what he likes

Except make the audience care
Step in the club and then bogart the joint
They hold me in lowly regard
Get threatened with sticks and keep missing the point
Hoist on my own petard
Thence to return and repeat and rehash
To hunt for what magic I missed
Whilst busily running a hundred-year dash,
The sentence a mill to my grist.
So it's Groundhog Day all over again
I end it just like I begin
By cloning old jokes with a giggling pen
Like Sisyphus' mischievous twin
Life is grim
Tories Out
Meditation's what it's all about
Sex is sex
Death is death
Words condensing in a wasted breath
Gripe gripe gripe
Rage rage rage
Same old shit on a different page
Kids are kids
Kent is Kent
Time is time until it gets misspent.
What's it all for, eh?
What's it all for?

I wrote while I commuted
Until my muse got neutered.
My wiped-out mind computed

It might be better suited
To indolent repose.
So welcome, wilkommen, bienvenue,
See what obsession and boredom can do.
Tread dead water for a year or two,
Watch a dead body of work accrue,
Then push -
      - Away it goes.

Other People Are Just The Worst

The Awful People Show

Oh she's unnecessary,
She wishes people harm.
She looks like Grayson Perry
But doesn't have his charm.
She lets her thoughts meander;
She only changes mind
When fed some propaganda
To hitch her hate behind.
Thus she works out what to do
To folk she does not know.
Welcome welcome welcome to
The awful people show.

Oh he's unnecessary,
He wishes people death.
He looks like Mary Berry
But jacked on crystal meth.
All gimlet bullet eyeball glint
And teeth ground down and out,

He'll show you the excuse in print
For knocking you about.
When you see him stroll up,
That's your cue to go -
Roll up, roll up, roll up,
It's the awful people show.

Anyone, at no expense,
Can get less unenlightened.
It makes no difference if you're dense,
Only if you're frightened.
People act like little shits
Then revel in their goofs,
But which are worse - the hypocrites,
Or killers telling truths?
But this is stuff that makes me sick;
Do as you'd have so,
And all the rest is rhetoric -
An awful people show.

I'm bitter, I am twisted,
But what do you expect?
My precious plans got fisted
And turned out incorrect.
I fall foul, it must appear,
Of what I criticise.
Forgive me if I'm insincere
When I apologise.
If I cannot fully win,
I'll drag the world below
And we'll all take our places in

The awful people show.

"Wilkommen, bienvenue, welcome
Im Cabaret, au Cabaret, to Cabaret"

The Flow of Losers Never Stops

The flow of losers never stops.
O'er the hillside, here they come.
Blithe, into your bed each hops.
Where do you get these losers from?
I find myself become a judge;
Their quality is always dire.
The quantity I don't begrudge -
The quantity, I quite admire.
I do not prematurely froth;
They give me cause to think them worse:
The things they do to piss you off,
The things they say when we converse.
They were not born to loserdom
But studied hard at misbehaviour.
Then, their loser status won,
Lay in wait to gain your favour.

Does one visit loser shops,
Where dismal queue meets dismal queue?
Stood in one line, human slops;
Stood within the other, you?
Are there loser superstores?
SuperLoserMetroMart,

Where aisles of loser men are yours
For stuffing in your shopping cart?
You could not meet them where you work;
You could not meet them where you learn,
For risk such concentrated jerk
Implode themselves through self-concern.
And this was twenty years ago!
You were no computer user.
Twenty years from then, you'd know
The joys of Tindr, Grindr, Losr.

I too was a loser once,
But married, grew, and re-acquitted.
Faced with these insipid twunts
I might have found myself embittered.
Now, chagrinned, askance, bemused,
Bestow I prayers to goodness knows.
Of all the lovers you perused,
These ones were the ones you chose?
Still, I've no right but to concur;
Trust, I must, what you prefer,
Hoping that these wretched men,
Lost once, might be lost again.

Gaslight

History is one damn thing
After another, after another
Why is yours worth favouring
Over another, over another?

Gaslight
Memories are hues with which he paints.
Gaslight
You're the story he manipulates.
Gaslight. How surprising,
The things that you forgot.
Gaslight
You and he. Which one lost the plot?

So you convene a court for me
Where scale of justice represents
Both balance and severity,
And every wrong needs recompense.
You stand to make the case:
His lies have brought about
Intolerable doubt.
You fling it in his face and then
Another case is built

On pretty much the same again,
Intolerable guilt.
For years you sit, both mute, aloof
Where once you sat allied,
As if there were some magic truth
To gauge yourselves beside.

Gaslight
Tell the world your story many times.
Gaslight
We listen listen listen to his crimes.
Gaslight
He made you fall for things that were not true.
Gaslight
What a thing for somebody to do.

If you're a step to step on,
Then war games must be played;
You scrabbled for a weapon,
And found one ready-made.
You name the liberties he took -
You call the thing *"gas-light"*.
It stalks you like the Babadook;
It only comes out at night.
It gives you needful things to hate,
Complete with hunting call.
The dawn sees them evaporate;
You long for night to fall.
Assertions and perversions
That he hurls out, pell mell,
You match with fresh incursions,

Oddly parallel,
With unilateral blame;
The biggest lie you tell is that your lies are not the same.
But this is no man's justice and a story must be told;
You judge your propaganda based on how the viewers polled.
Set some others testing him.
For longer than you knew him, you're
Invested in (but bested in)
Vampiric Pyrrhic war;
As long as light
Is strong, a slight
Will be slight hurt, no more,
But you are long haul travellers,
Dug in, dark and deep.
Night-time is for fighting in,
And, henceforth, none shall sleep.

Gaslight
I do not think you innocent of charge
Gaslight
I do not believe your reportage
Gaslight
You twist events just like you said he did
Gaslight
Go and find some other fool to kid.

Bathe beneath the midday sun.
Be yourself and be as one,
Where people are not things to fix,
And gaslight's naught but parlour tricks.

"He kinda shoulda sorta woulda loved her if he could've.
The story's getting closer to the end.
He kinda shoulda sorta woulda loved her if he could've.
He'd rather be alone than pretend."

I Spell Well

I spell well, I
Spell very well.
Read my letters; you can tell.
Yessir, I can spell.

I know all my phonics
I'm the best in town
I spell *"Economics"*;
I spell *"Trickle Down"*.
Spell well and I'm ecstatic,
And righteously am so.
Some words are problematic, but
My favourite word is *"No"*.

I can spell *"Redundant"*,
"Surplus", *"Unemployed"*.
I can spell the words that other
People might avoid.
I can spell impeccably
To fill in your pink slip.
I before E except after C,
Like in *"Receivership"*.
I can spell *"Subpoena"*,

I can spell *"Solicit"*,
"Injunction", *"Misdemeanour"*;
My spelling is exquisite.

When I see misspelling,
I feign astonishment
And act like there's no telling the
Authorial intent.
I can spell *"unsuitable"*,
In reference to you.
I spell *"unrecruitable"*,
And very often do.
You aren't what we were looking for;
Please do not re-apply.
You couldn't even spell in your
Curriculum Vitae.
You wrote of, in your slipshod screed,
The poor hand you were dealt.
My CV's a cracking read,
And very nicely spelt.

I run a tidy company,
And you may go to hell.
Thank God the CEO is me,
Not someone who can't spell.

The Lifeboats of your Small Affair

Close your eyes. Snuff the candle out.
Wish your woman well and unaware.
Lay the stakes of what this is about;
These are the lifeboats of your small affair.

Drink and find some friends to justify it;
Find some friends whom drink might justify
Tell your tale to anyone who'll buy it
Someone grateful when you say goodbye
Tiptoe out in 50 different ways
Tippex over any signs of care
Hang your head for days and days and days
These are the lifeboats of your sad affair

Run and leave a dummy in your stead
Find a likely shoulder for your yoke
Bequeath your love your empty heart and bed
Teach her how to take your funny joke
Stow yourself beyond the blackout blind
Find a new projectrix for your ire
Watch and see your motives undermined
Shudder, baulk and set your life on fire
Pretend the fault was anyone's but yours

Dwell on previous monogamies;
Only the successes, not the flaws
Magnify those failures but not these
Slather acid on your hands and face
Angle-grind your teeth and fingerprints
Nothing will sufficiently erase
The list of errors made before and since
Scuttle into infidelities
Take the very limit you can bear
Cut your losses, shuffle overseas
These are the lifeboats of your small affair

Shun whichever people you can blame
Blame whichever people you can shun
State the regulations of your game
Many stand to gain, but you're not one
Still you shoot, spectate, and referee
Then think your judgement lauded everywhere -
Demigodden, fair as fair can be;
These are the lifeboats of your small affair.

The danger, once you reach this end of days,
Is finding out your planning was for naught
And books of petty ploys, your poison plays,
Were not the rigid guarantees you'd thought
In icy oceans. Every muscle numbs,
And now your life relies upon your grip.
So hope some shining Lusitania comes;
Isn't she a pretty pretty ship?

The World Is Going To Hell In A Handcart Because Of The Right Wing

Be My Tory Wife

Well I tried to be affectionate
To my plebian electorate
But scraped through when the pushing came to shove
I wanted to be fêted
But wound up tolerated
I won their votes but could not win their love

For when I doorstep, they can see
I have a female vacancy
And need some frau to occupy my life
I can be your geezer
And you'll be my Theresa
Be my be my be my Tory wife

Be my Tory wife
Be my Tory spouse, be
Suitably expensive and I'll claim you like my house
Plus my Mayfair flat
You can be my chattel

And back me up in battle
And that'll be the living end of that

Well I'll make it worth your while
If you'll fake a little smile
And pretend I'm not as awful as I am
All comforts are afforded
You'll be suitably rewarded
If you overlook my sordid little sham

I'm a scheming overreacher
A sleazy Friedrich Nietzsche
Who oversees the DWP
Beget me Tory kids
Or I'll stop your benefits
I certify you fit to work on me

Accept you're second fiddle
Accept my sprawling middle
Accept that I'll be bigoted and weird
Accept that I'll be heinous
Accept my latent gayness
Accept that you'll be living as my beard

I'll teach you to be wary at
The sight of proletariat
And duck when something wicked this way comes
You can fluster fragrantly
And I can bluster flagrantly
And do that really strange thing with my thumbs

The only skills you need
Are hiding where you bleed
And creeping slowly, brandishing your knife
So when the time befits
We will stab our fellow shits
And then you'll be a Tory PM's wif-f-f-f-f-fe.

A Land Grab by the Useless

Observe: The application of free market economics to our system of government. Whosoever provides the most superficially attractive bid for an unpopular service is awarded the contract.

Hot potato,
Hot potato,
Pass it on, it's a hot potato,
Careful, very hot.

You grabbed the poison chalice and you asked it be refilled
They topped it up and over and the liquor overspilled
It dripped its bitter ooze
On someone else's shoes
You lost your reputation but that's nothing much to lose
And nothing to rebuild.
Join the backbenchers
Filthy as the Ganges,
The phalanx of twats.
You love to join phalanges
Of putrid bureaucrats.
Different now than then;

The men of way-back-whenadays
Became the kind of senseless
Schmucker that you'd find
While watching The Apprentice
Or maybe Dragon's Den.
Unconcerned with learning;
Your schooling's inextensive.
You did not go to Eton
Just some comprehensive, so
You think the system's beaten
And anyone who isn't in your little field of view
Cannot have spent their effort half as wisely as did you.
They did not have the sense
To tread your well-trod ground;
To sell for 99 full pence
What might be worth a pound.
Cite your scant beginnings
Flat cap, school bag, chips and peas for dinner
Compare it with your winnings
Clearly you're a winner
And thus this qualifies
For one free easy ride
But, to external eyes,
You self-disqualified
By filching out a fortune
From those less fortunate
You grabbed your neighbour's portion
And broke off half their plate.
Craning, straining goldfish eyes,
Knock-kneed when the stocks go bullish,
You act all tough and pennywise

But billion-pound foolish.
Self-made by a hobbyist
Who threw away the mould,
You grovel to the lobbyist,
For product must be sold.
You lucked out; your mobility
Somehow left you spared.
Simper to nobility;
The feeling is not shared.
Here's the Tory fallacy:
Anyone can succeed
Does not imply
Everyone can succeed.
For any definitions.
For any circumstances.
For even politicians are
Results of sets of chances.
There's a reason you got what you wanted;
It went unwanted.

Sleepwalk up the echelons,
You undeserving mob
Of toryboy automatons,
Learning on the job.
You lullabied our troops
To sleep with your obtuseness; it's
A land grab by the useless,
A coup by nincompoops.

The Al Capone of Downing Street

[Those of you who remember who David Cameron was might also remember that he got into hot water over non-payment of some tax or other. It seemed strange to me that he would get into trouble over this, instead of getting into trouble over sodding the country right up, and it reminded me of quite another historical figure]

"Say, that's a nice welfare state you got there.
Be a shame if anything...happened to it."

Cruising round the corner,
The Conservative Camorra.
Call the cops, it's Dodgy Dave,
In trenchcoat and fedora.
He will steal the stuff you own
And sell you off like meat,
For David is our Al Capone,
Down in Downing Street.

The underworld big cheeses
Fill Westminster speakeasies
To plot against the weak.
They refrain from making change;

It's easier to speak.
If your view's a Commie one,
Hang on to your Tommy gun;
Keep it handy, pal.
Always pack some heat.
One day you might meet the Al
Capone of Downing Street.

He's running a farrago
As if it were a mission.
The House of Commons recently
Is Golden-Age Chicago,
But with a prohibition
On basic human decency.
Little Nick Clegg had an accident;
No-one knew where the poor guy went.
He fell into the Thames
While wearing concrete slippers -
A warning shot for all Lib-Dems,
A gift for all UKIPpers.
Statesmen with the pathos
Of Saturday cartoons
Pay musclemen like ATOS
To be their hired goons;
Debt-collecting heavies
In search of skulls to crack
Go levy proxy levies
On those who can't fight back.
Send you round some visitors
Who'll force you into penance.
Baseball bat inquisitors,

The IDS lieutenants,
Sneak up in crêpe-soled shoes.
They fill the public coffers
By making paupers offers
That they may not refuse.
Scarfing Bob Terwillingers
Drip us steaming slops.
They think they're the cream of crops.
They think they're ninja Dillingers,
But they're the Keystone Cops.
They run when the press come knocking;
They shroud themselves in stocking
And what cover they can get.
They hide in shady places;
The shadows mask their faces
From the shadow cabinet.
The darkness dims their sins,
And in their case, their cases
Hold actual violins.
They play Tchaikovsky softly
To soothe the mewling proles.
This fails, of course, but soothes remorse
In their own makeshift souls.

And who's the pick of the toothless grins?
The biggest prick of the new kingpins?
It's Scarface Dave and his scar's his smile.
Watch him smirk as he stands on trial
At Awkward Question Time;
A game he will not lose.
Deny your crime at PMQs;

Ride out the abuse. Meanwhile,
Nothing much ensues.
Scream at the heathen *"Confess, confess!*
You ordered the hit on the NHS!"
But he will never confess
With Jeremy Corbyn as Eliot Ness;
All the restraint of a painted saint.
"Is it your fault, this austerity mess?"
"Well...maybe it is, and...maybe it ain't."
He's cost the nation packets.
It's fiscally unsound
To run protection rackets
The other way around;
To bribe his friends the bankers
To help the poor stay poor;
To meekly thank the thankless
And send our funds offshore.
Somehow it's irrelevant his state is at its knees;
Somehow it's irrelevant his rich get all the cheese;
Somehow it's irrelevant his actions snub the facts;
The only thing that's relevant is: Did he fudge his tax?
Did he really evade or not?
I don't care if he paid or not;
I don't care if he made a plot;
All that matters is he got got,
And when the man's comeuppance comes
It will be sweet as candied plums
For Al Capone was born to fail,
And Dave will taste defeat;
We'll send him to San Quentin jail
Instead of Downing Street.

On the Eve of the Inauguration

On the eve of the inauguration,
The drunkard dragged up to the stage.
(Open mics are a blessing,
Open mics are a curse)
He fumed with a great indignation
And built to a murderous rage,
Shouting about how we make him feel sick
(Freedom of speech
Means freedom also to ignore you)
Then gifted us half of a lewd limerick -
Two and a quarter full lines.
"What about Trump? What about Trump?"
As if he had barely crossed our minds,
Left through the ear he entered in,
Over our heads with a hop and a jump,
Never to speak of again.
What pithy insight might fanfaring come,
Valiantly sprung from my head?
(Poetry is the last refuge of the scoundrel)
As if there were any a depth to plumb,
And something were still left unsaid.

Alas, I replied, my notebook is blank;
Blow your own rallying trumpet.
(Insert words here,
Where "Here" is "Up your fundament")
I've written my fill of embittered old wank;

You'll have what you're given, and lump it.
Do you despair at my POTUS-shaped hole,
Freed from all shrieking reports?
Never to worry, you sweet precious soul,
The world is repeating your thoughts.
Ask me to write what I'd rather forget?
You bid me be shallow and deep.
(Ars gratia arseholes)
Look, and you'll find there's a whole internet
Who'll endlessly yell you to sleep.
YouTube is full of the sorry-not-sorry,
Shocking themselves with their nerve.
(Everyone is anonymous on the internet,
Except for those who should be)
Facebook has landed a suitable quarry,
Memes got the foe they deserve.
Repeat and repeat and mutate and repeat,
Shutting the stable door
After the horse has but there is no stable here
And no door
And the horse is in DC
The ostlers are overseas
And the stable is in downtown Manhattan.

Bring Me Your Children, Ulysses Grant

Bring me your children, Ulysses Grant
Bring me your troublesome sons
Some are worth saving but some of them aren't
And those are the dangerous ones

I'll see that they're schooled in the word of the Lord
Where shepherded families belong
For youngsters need something for shoving toward
Away from all secular wrong

How will I heal them? I'll tsk and I'll tut
And wish that some deeds were undone.
As for some action? Well, anything but;
Let's not go jumping the gun.

Birthrights, God-given, may never be stripped
So live with their outcomes or die
And see the good people are fully equipped
For taking an eye for an eye

Heavens, it makes me selectively proud;
This land bent on purging its sin
Where Numbers and Letters are only allowed
Depending which Book they are in.

Ayn Rand Christmas

Do not think that friends or kin
Are things that one would wish to keep
In contact with, or welcome in.
Do your Yuletide on the cheap.
Sit around no Christmas tree.
Have no wasteful cards displayed.
It saps the timber industry.
It props up ailing paper trade.
Lay your dollar bills in rows
And fasten them in joyful chains,
So when the twelfth night comes and goes,
All that matters still remains.
Wealth is righteous. Understand,
Good need not be pleasant.
Merry Christmas, love, Ayn Rand;
Keep your lousy present.

If guests should catch you unawares,
Dress as Scrooge in festive black.
Give them coal and steal it back,
Then tell them that the fault was theirs.
Bill them once for Christmas pud;
Bill them twice for Christmas crackers.

'Tis the time when greed is good,
So twist them firmly by the knackers.
Ain't it funny, ain't it grand,
Isn't life a treat?
Merry Christmas, love Ayn Rand -
Please don't take a seat.

Santa is a Communist.
When will children learn?
There is no nice or naughty list -
Get a job and earn.
He's got some kind of Latin name,
Maybe Venezuelan.
Shoot that punk like deer or game;
Pretend you're Sarah Palin.
"Santa Claus is here again!",
Sing the children's choir.
Take their letters, sayeth Ayn,
And place them on the fire.

If you live in Bethlehem
And find some Nazarene
Comes begging you to welcome them,
A homeless pregnant teen,
Ditch that scrounging Mary and baby,
Show them that you care.
Be a libertarian, baby,
Make them sleep elsewhere.

Still your itching helping hand;
Do not be a mug.
Love is harsh, thus spake Ayn Rand.
Act like Atlas: Shrug.

Trickle-Down Nice

Something wrong has happened here,
Amid the grave estates.
The property got uppity
And went and upped its rates.
The squatters got blind-sided;
Their squats got gentrified.
They could not buy, like I did,
So now they squat outside.
The up-and-coming rotten town
Lures wealth by strange device.
The money doesn't trickle down;
What trickles down is *Nice*.

The swish-posh malls have greeters
Who grin, as if they care,
Through phoney gritted features,
But *we* know why they're there -
To act as human barriers;
Keep-out-people gates.
They let in gold-card carriers,
But not the reprobates.
"*You* do not deserve of *this*,
Nor *you* deserve of *these*."

A glimpse of all the Nice they miss
Trickles out to tease,
Through one-way glass whose one way is
The way those inside please.

The bankers paint their frontage
With Nutcracker vignettes,
Which must seem pretty cuntish
To those the world forgets.
The shops have cosy porticos
Festooned with fairy lights
To fill you full of ho-ho-hos
On stony winter nights,
While sleeping tight in boxes
Of quite a finer style.
They're thick, and keep the foxes
Outside your domicile.
Write a funny sign out front.
Passers-by will flip a little
Trickle-down smile.

They hung up stars of Bethlehem;
The neon heavens glow.
Those who languish under them
Freeze hellishly below.
Someone somewhere did the maths
And found the megawatts
Would better entertain the Haves
Than heat up the Have-Nots.
Rescuing a lowly few
Is barely worth the price,

But *everyone* enjoys the view.
Trickle-down nice.

England's built on finer things
Than handouts to the poor.
Thusly spake our Tory kings,
Laying down the law.
Beggars do not get a taste,
Like they were you or I.
Everybody hates a waste.
Once Britain, twice shy.
All must work to earn their slice.
While you wait for pie, here:
Trickle-down nice.

One fine day, a councilman
Will take some vagrant by the hand
And lead them to the street they used to sleep on
Saying, *Look:*
Isn't it so much nicer
Now you're not on it?

Is It OK To Punch A Nazi?

With a shining side-parting
And a cleanly shorn chin
He thinks he's firestarting
He thinks that he'll win
He's a casual gamer
Who likes to play Risk
He's a false flag inflamer
He'll burn you a disk
He's a sulphur igniter
An alpha drum beater
A phoney foe fighter
A phantom defeater
A face full of odium
And a futon HQ
One foot on the podium
And one foot on you
A rhetorical filigree
Conducting a class
He's a walking soliloquy
Who sits on his arse
He's a bug in the system
A twunt saboteur
A fount of all wisdom -

Would that he were.
He's a blood-sucking leech,
A scum-sucking bore
Crying *"Freedom of speech!"*,
Like that's what it's for.
He pimps out his selfie
And sucks from the pump
Held out by the wealthy
He wants to gazump.
He thinks that it's healthy
To gorge and then dump;
Adolf is his Delphi,
His calling-card, Trump.

They say on YouTube he destroys,
But I see no destruction.
He's like a hoover making noise
Without creating suction.
Whiter still and whiter,
He speaks in hieroglpyhs.
He's a Blighty blighter;
Throw him off our cliffs.
Don't get bleeding-heartsy,
Do not second-guess.
Can you punch a Nazi?
Yes, Virginia, yes.

Love Your Local Nazi

If you know some failure
Who dresses in regalia
Like brown shirts, jackboots, caps and lederhosen
And if the chap confesses
They'd like to join the S.S.,
Then help them off the path that they have chosen

OH

Love love love love love your local Nazi
Demonstrate a better way to live
Make them feel beloved
Snuggled, hugged and smothered
Give what Daddy Adolf did not give, yes
Love love love love love your local Nazi,
For are we not, we brotherhood, alike?
End our silly quarrels
Teach them proper morals
Show it isn't true that might is Reich
Deck their house with tinsel
Abnegate their crimes
If they are an incel
Incelebrate good times!

Go and play some frisbee
With some Sephardim
Watch some nice Walt Disney
Wait, hang on, not him. Do you
Cruise in a bunch?
No no no
Crunch and a bruise?
No no no
Juice in the punch?
OK yes
Punching the Jews?
No no no, SO
Love love love love love love your local Nazi
Steer them from a path they might regret
And as your heart embiggens you can be their Henry Higgins
Teach them proper speech and etiquette, yes,
I contend, befriend your local Nazi
Skip beside them, hand in leather glove
Make your contribution
A kind of restitution, for the
Final solution's always love.

Tree-Hugging Hippy Crap

Focus on the Breath

What is with me when I sit,
Never to be rid of it?
What makes its presence felt by touch,
Not too little, not too much?
What is faint but yet precise?
What is ever close at hand?
What is right before your eyes,
Only half at your command?

As I kneel to meditate
Focus on the breath
Turn the dial to "Concentrate"
Focus on the breath
Inner quiet, inner still,
Exercise an iron will.
Though it be a bitter pill,
Focus on the breath

As I feel my focus drift
Focus on the breath
As I feel perception shift

Focus on the breath
As I hear subconscious hum
As I feel my buttocks numb
As I seethe in tedium
Focus on the breath

You need not to be the breath,
Just perceive it being.
If you do not see the breath,
What, then, are you seeing?

As I grind my gritted teeth
Focus on the breath
As I simmer underneath
Focus on the breath
As I feel the pressure grow
As I feel the pleasure glow
As above, so then below
Focus on the breath

As I rise and as I fall,
Focus on the breath.
Though my mind disguise it all,
Focus on the breath.
As I kneel and as I itch,
As I keel and as I pitch,
As I squeal and as I bitch,
Focus on the breath

Allow myself a little doubt.
Laugh,

Focus is enough.
Breathe in, breathe out.
Wax on, wax off.

As I drool at Pavlov's bell
Focus on the breath
Focus tolerably well
Focus on the breath
As my mind go hula-hoop
As I run an endless loop
As my monologues regroup
Focus on the breath

Though it bore me half to death
Focus on the breath
As I focus on the breath
Focus on the breath
Do not control the breath.
Focus.
Only behold the breath.
Focus.

Like a clock whose minutes
Repeat at different hours,
But with an inner difference.
What, then, is yours?
A set of rules without a game.
Effect beside the cause.
A pointless quest without an aim;
No things for aiming at.
Nothing there to master,

Treat imposters just the same.
Triumph and disaster, and all that.

Grab the Buddha by the throat
Focus on the breath
Strangulate the little scrote
Focus on the breath
Though he be inscrutable,
Though he glow full beautiful,
He by my boot be bootable -
But focus on the breath

Let your senses be your guides,
But not the type you trust.
They will beg believe their lies;
Do not feel you must.
Every second subdivides
In several respects.
Fill each fraction subdivision
Full of your attention,
Full of your inaction;
Move on to the next.

As I try and fail to keep
Focus on the breath
As I lie and fail to sleep,
Focus on the breath
Be you pauper, be you king,
Be you boss or underling,
Focus on the focussing.
Focus is the thing, boys,

Focus on the breath.

As I feel impermanence,
Focus on the breath.
As I undermine my sense,
Focus on the breath.
Other pain has gone long since;
All this too shall pass,
Like rain erasing fingerprints
Left upon the glass.

It Is An Emptiness

It is an emptiness
That slowly fills. You tip
And wait and tip again,
Look it in the eye. It will not stay.
The waters rise,
Churning surfs about.
There are squalls, qualia,
Hushed by a firm hand,
       mute threats.
The asymptotes evaporate;
Lather, rinse, repeat.
Each time, strive, tire,
Bow before defeat.

Dull Eyes

Dull eyes
I will cultivate dull eyes
Look like a bull shark
Holding love inside
Dull eyes
I am not prey
Dull eyes don't see problems
The problems run away

Peeps shall view my quickening
Trembling, and scare
That is quite the type of thing
For which I will not care
Come the triumph, come disaster
Sit I still as Paris plaster

Dull eyes; eyes so dull
Growing ever masterful
Shineless iris hides no glitter
Deadeye bullseye target hitter
Wastes no time in sizing up
Concomitant threats
Qualia come rising up

Stemming from regrets
Tiger's strike or leaf in fall
Each alike, alike in all
Dull eyes
Tend my dull eyes
And as I let my muscles go
My brow shall hang, unfurrowed, low
Shrouding my bedulled
        brown
                eyes

When I'm Enlightened

When I'm enlightened
I will be thin
I'll conquer my craving
For whisky and gin
I won't feel all needful
Of pudding or pies
And I'll sit in full lotus
With sleek skinny thighs
And it's no nay never
No nay never no more
Shall I bow to attachments
No never no more

The women will love me
They'll giggle and stare;
I'll sit all enraptured
With nary a care
Sweet Spanish ladies
May fondle me cheek
But I'll grin benignly
And will not grow weak
For it's no nay never
No nay never again

To my earthly attachments
For they are in vain

I'll glow in transcendence
Of Heaven and Hell
I'll write books about it
And smile when they sell
I'll spend all the proceeds
On mony a thing
Build my own ashram
And rule as its king
For it's no nay never
No nay never nohow
To my earthly attachments
For I'm better than thou

Brenda Wants A Buddha

Brenda wants a Buddha
To make her feelings finer
Tescos sells them ten a penny
Each one made in China
Each with matching nomenclature
Each the shade of grout
Each of them with Buddha-nature
Each of them without

Where coulda Buddha be downset,
To lend his benefices?
Near the water featurette,
Where my youngest pisses?
By the lichened sparrow bath?
On my eightfold garden path?
Out beside the patio
In silent diorama?
Tell me, where should Buddha go
To preach a speechless dharma?

From such stuff as Buddha hates,
Forms of him consist:
Permanence and aggregates,

Concepts he dismissed.
Though I love the ornamental -
Though I love the Oriental -
Statuary won't suffice
To tame my shameful Western vice.
Idols, while a quiet reminder
What you do can be done kinder,
Will not teach you any more
Than what you had not learnt before.
As the master's koan said:
If you, on your travel,
Meet the Buddha, strike him dead;
Grind him into gravel.

Doomed Love

Two Doomed Loves

I was precocious. At the age of eight
I defended her honour
      and the honour of her coat,
          which other boys said looked like a bin bag.
I, meanwhile,
      developed a fetish
          for PVC.
We both played piano -
      The Snowman -
          - *WE'RE WALKING IN THE AIR* -
She one transcription, I another.
This confused me;
      Why transcribe it twice?
I held both pedals down,
      because pedals were magic.
She was grade something, I was not.
Also, she played the harp.
With twelve pedals, the harp
      is four or six times as magic
      as a piano.

I took up guitar,
    and doomed myself to solipsism.

I dreamt one day
    we would live in Madagascar
        (because of its abundant natural resources)
In a great glass pyramid
    made of one-way mirrors
        (for privacy),
Swathed in vines on every side.
All would be green light and nude joy -
    Well, I said I was precocious.
She reluctantly received
    my first sonnet,
Presented with a golden butterfly
    bought at the Commonwealth Centre
        for fifty pence
        while my mother was distracted.
The sonnet asked she be discreet.
    Perhaps she was;
    I doubt it.
She was eventually seduced
    by an erstwhile friend;
    the Quilty to my Humbert Humbert,
A quisling bitch
    who claimed Michael Jackson
    as a close personal confidant.
He fumbled with her
    in a public swimming pool.
Their ineptitudes were widely reported.
We parted at eleven,

she to an all-girls school
   and I a mixed one,
A triumph of my hope
      over her experience.
After that, we met rarely.

Music was my longest love
And gave me all that it could give.
I gave it all I felt like giving;
Barely half enough.
Now I blush each time we meet
Or hear it praised by common friends.
We see each other some weekends;
Pass like strangers in the street.

Meanwhile,
I found out what she had been doing
      with her life.

She grew, produced some TV shows,
Became some great success
And lived for music. So it goes;
I came to less and less.
So now my feckless TV screen
Bestows her little gifts,
As if it were a go-between
That works in yearly shifts.
I sit alone, oh woe is me,
With ever-cooling ardours,
And she records the bonhomie
Of comrade promenaders.

She broadcasts from the Albert Hall
The concerts I attended,
Before such things meant bugger all
And I became unmended.
Two passions, dropped adrift and died,
Shine unto empty eyes;
Sent with love, but cast aside,
Like golden butterflies.

I Wrote For You Then And I Write For You Now

I wrote for you then and I write for you now,
O butt of my former misdeeds
Whom I could not trust with a why or a how
Personas or motives or needs
Who handily bent to the plans that I made
Until those same plans were enacted
Then thenceforth whose shimmering chimera's shade
Was whitewashed, reworked and redacted

Your virtues were many but none of them fixed
O girl of the plasticine face
So each time I begged to be mocked and deep-sixed
There was little of note to replace
I fashioned you large and I fashioned you small
In Lego and string and K'nex
With nothing remaining consistent at all
Aside from our putative sex
And all efforts took I to make you my own
Excepting the medium of talk
And patterned around you a fuckable zone
An archery target in chalk

But now I'm an adult, the taxman supposes
Which may be the case, at a push
I now have no need of my fair English roses
And leave them in bloom on the bush
As if they were people, not variant themes
Fey fractals extracted from seeds
All nurtured in service of slovenly dreams
So please to forgive -
        Please not to relive -
My formative years and misdeeds.

When I Lied

What I wanted came to be
When I lied
Time stood still and so did she
When I lied
I held her hand and held her gaze
When I lied
And warped the world's most precious phrase
When I lied

What should have been my blossoming
Became a misbegotten thing;
A sin to which my thoughts might cling,
When I lied.
Her kiss was given unto me
When I lied and bastardised its legacy
When I lied.
My question lay without my voice
Forever petrified;
Why was I to be her choice?
So,
I lied.

Time is spent for time is cheap

When youth is in its flush
So gamble what you cannot keep
And tell yourself, hush hush,
Go act as if your thoughts are pure
And keep your motives hid;
For I would lie for so much more,
And did.

Good God You've Grown Up

Good God you've grown up.
Your naked arse on Facebook,
Poised with a grace
You didn't have when younger.
You say your husband likes the picture,
Well,
No fooling.
What can I do with this image?
Not what I would have done once.
Whistle, cheer? I'll do it. I could.
Further back, photos.
Your sweet daughter;
I, the age of you,
She, the age of my eldest,
And every year, two Happy Birthdays
On the same day. It reminds us.
Once, at a specific age,
I nearly almost said:

> *"Today is our last chance*
> *To lose our virginities illegally"*

But worried you'd reply:

> " *Well,*
>
> *Perhaps for* you".

So, like when I asked you out,
It passed as nothing.
University years,
Wherever they were spent.
Moving to towns in a county in the country.
Now we reacquaint,
In manners of speaking.
Proxy friends, Facebook.
I read about your problems. Real-world shit.
You walk on,
Sweet daughter,
Arse on Facebook.
Go girl, I'm fine,
Broadly. It's not all bad.

As I age, I understand
Why men keep women veiled
Their bodies are a reprimand
For all the ways I've failed
To get the things I always craved.
Slowly, I was taught
That somehow I had misbehaved,
Not doing as I ought,
And if you were what I required
I never should have said,
For now I've seen what I desired
Through silences instead.

I Should Have Savoured You Like A Fine Wine

I should have savoured you like a fine wine.
I should have listened, should have learned.
The secrets in your libraries
Were checked out blindly, then returned,
Unseen as if a Ulysses;
The clues were there, but masked.
Laid out open, had I pleased;
But then, I never asked.

I suffered at the hands of hands;
Mangled keys in rusted locks,
And all of me was hinterlands
In constant states of static shocks.
I could not take a simple kiss,
So much less that much more,
That fixing what we found amiss
Became a decade's war.
Our trystings were a tasting note,
The schema of your scent,
Which stuck and stung my baby's throat
In ways that were not meant.
And while our love was friendship, fate

Decreed I leave it doomed;
For all we did was consummate,
And I was unconsumed.

Excommunication

This is an excommunication
It has ceased to be
It is the choir invisible
Meaningless to me

An excommunication
From exes long ago
Telling me the many things
I'd rather never know

Wheeled into a full light
Goaded then released
My fabled papal bullfight
Hanged, harangued, deceased

Bittersour, a Judas kiss
The Inquisition's writ
Painful when they fire and miss
Painful when they hit

A tacit condemnation
Held within my head
An ex-communication
Dead Dead Dead Dead Dead.

wat

Ebbsfleet Internal

Contradiction tradition:
Hardness, lightheartedness,
Hypothetically poetically.

Departmentalising parenting:
Minions' determinations,
Insubordination urination;
Relation reconciliation.

Possess postmistresses
Enthusiastically, ethically,
Taking thanksgiving.

Photosensitive positive.
Scientific: scenic,
Unsuccessful, useful.

Comment commencement:
Fiction specification;
Reenter screenwriters.

Protein protectiveness:
Movement impoverishment,
Action cancellation;
Stoically, asymtotically,
Motion harmonisation.

Analog scandalmonger,
Princes' presidencies.
Scandalmonger scanner,
Scandalmonger danger!
Interrogated, iterated,
Investigation negation,
Auction malfunction!
Fiction simplification.

Novice nonviolence -
Schoolteacher shooter,
Master manslaughter.

Strenuous, tenuous, disadvantageous savage.
Morality manoeuvrability:
Neutralisation elision,
Uncompromising uprising,
Hanging thanksgiving.

Betterer and Betterer

Thank God last year's over.
Also, April, May,
Yesterday's lethargy.
Caring less for yesterdays,
I find atoning boring,
Getting less atoney as I go.
I'm too old for *if only*;
If only that were so.

Who's the me I'm kidding?
Sums of lazy doubts,
Apathetically bidding
Indeterminate amounts
On random hands of poker.
Everything is meh, yeh?
All is mediocre.

Minimise my maxims, preach
To me, save time
By knowing what I teach
Already. I'm
A self-devised
Textbook, therefore, handily,

I'm fully self-revised.
Neither scrimp nor gluttonise;
Take the third way,
Building flimsy alibis
With masquerades and wordplay.
Have I no shame?
Yes, no.
No, yes.
Disguise my hurts
With sarcasm,
Long-sleeved shirts
And pleonasm.
We're a funny lot;
Struggle to stay warm
Without becoming overhot.
Super stupid nuts are we,
Writers on the storm.
Bitter weeds,
Battered wrecks -
Wrack reeks the seabed.
Sunk last week
And rose the next.
See, all is
Ebb and flow,
Sliced in stasis.
Never know the
Timings. See, some
      times things become
Betterer and betterer,
Etcetera etcetera.

Sleep Object

Sleep object.
Twist it round;
Will it fit,
Beside the other
Sleep objects?
A Tetris froth,
A Rubik's foam.
Pudgy fractal jigsaw
Threatens to disperse
But doesn't.
I lack its match
A single cell
Porous ovum
Afterglows-shade.
Doorstepping phytoplankton
Fake news infection
Quiz show neon
Ding dong,
Sleep object.
I brought a thousand friends;
A Foreign Legion
The hues of sick avocados.
Wake up,

Time to sleep.

Roads from Trains

At nexuses that never meet,
The railway joins a stubbed-out street;
Available, by happenstance,
To insectile pedestriants.
Unbarriered, I slip aboard
And fly myself along the line,
The copper cord,
The iron twine
In sideways freefall slip abroad.
Projected outwards by the eyes
We watch the world like little fish
As all its weft spaghettifies,
And wraps and sticks like liquorice
Awash with new topologies
That flee before they stake a stitch
And tempt me, *"Meld all those to these -*
Too late! Now tell me, which was which?"
Like plaster trails on slanted tiles
They birth opaque and bright and wet
But cross oblique like slats on stiles
And drip and fade before they set.

The streetlights from the underpass;

The bridges from the waterways;
The next semester from the last;
The noontides from the ends of days.

Roads from trains
Roads from trains
The world in your eyes.
Roads from trains
Roads from trains
Other people's lives.

The web of a gargantuan
Distracted spider. Disaffected,
Too dense to climb.
Lax and slack in vales, noodles
Hitherthither, at set heights,
Parallelipiped strata, lopes
Approximately orthogonally
County to county, shire to shire,
Cortèged in its tarmacadamed wake
By itself, laying steel
Prefab turds.

Men on far horizons wave;
They semaphore theodolites
And sit themselves in crosshaired sights
Until their shaking aim behaves.
Foci to loci,
Hocus pocus.
Loci to foci,
Hoc est corpus.

Points on curves and marks on graphs,
Emergent tangents, radii,
Elapse in sets of missing halfs
Beyond the ken of little I.

Clouds from planes,
Earth from air.
Roads from trains.
Then from now
And here from there.

...cummings ist der dichter...

Pickmeupas thoufyndestme,
  Prostrated scatteredy,
    He comes, he comes!
HE who quoth what mote it be,
  The soothdescriber!
  The downlawlayer!
  The boddhisattva once-returner!
Snows on hills bedeaden steps.
Far bells approach
  in tintinambulation,
    horsehoofs hiehence.
His rages augur august graces;
  Trojan strata trace gradations.
  Gasexpansive asterstasis
  Falls upon our favoured nations.
Pupilled of sweet mastery,
  Fern-curlicued arboreally,
  And, by turns, fullnastily,
  As twists itself in echolally.
The trumpet shall sound! The marimba shall sound!
The water-gong shall sound! The rototom shall sound!
  FLASH dun dun dun dun dun AH-AAAAAH
  HESAMIRACLE

Wo? Wo bist der dichter?
Cummings. Cummings ist der dichter.
Tattoo it on your arse,
    "*Jesus is coming, look busy*"

Starter Motor

Crank the handle
Rip the cord
Speak the magic wizard word
Kick the starter motor
Spark a stutter
Grind the rotor
Ride the sputter
Pray for lift
Shift the gears
Unbrake the brake
Unclutch the clutch
Rev, release
3 2 1 2 3 2 1 2 3 4 5

I try to stop.
I try to stop trying.
Stop trying! -
You are trying to stop.

I start and then
It seems OK, and then,
Oh, words. Familial thanksgivings,
Sibling affiliations.

See my mind? Trip it up,
But all I have for rope
Is mind. Give me
Barbed-wire clothesline
And two trees.

Rendered deafened, ear defenders
Set a buzzsaw shriking into
Vibrant silence, fizzing salience,
Alka-Seltzer proprioception.

Sped, the lights blur slowly.
Close my eyes, they twitch,
Dogs in a bag.
Plug my ears, heart
Pumping nervous chatter.

Each point a focus for
Its own amnesia, each
Blunders back. Lead weight,
Wet paper sack.

There it is there is it there it is
It it it
It is it is
T T T
Rusty gear chain teeth
Trapezoid wheel, fatiguing springs,
A disbelief of suspension.

The grit beneath my eyelid
Is fine, as long
As I not move.
A monkey trap; boxed bananas,
Razors round the hole.

I brace against the need to brace.
All is faded playground chalk
In dimming evening light,
And I am Orville Wright, at Kitty Hawk.

Miniatures

Dishwasher Chess

Pan to King's Pan 5.
Blackking casseroles.
Knife to Clean 4, fork.
Pan takes Dish up, en passata.
White takes black,
Plate in 3.

Vim Hymn

kjhlddp
Up down left right cut and paste
Everything's a shortcut key
Not a motion goes to waste

Span Song

Lovely
Super
Superlative
Super
Wonderful
Super(etc.)

One-Line Poem

"These condoms smell of scented nappy bags"

Tories

The only difference
    between
        a Tory
    and
        a Lavatory
    is
        the Direction.

In the Navy

At one point
I considered joining
Her Majesty's Navy.
When interviewed
By the recruiting officer,
I asked about the
    "Rum, sodomy and the lash",
But was told that
I would be on
The receiving end.

Don't Stand So Close To Sting

He knew not what he spoke of
And mispronounced "Nabokov"

Minims

I have fallen asleep on my keyboard.
Fortunately,
I am a minimalist composer
In the middle of a concert.

Heresy

Memento Mori

I

The ribs of wrecks play hide-and-seek
Along a sinusoidal scheme
Of fourteen cycles to the week;
As dips the moon, so lifts the beam.
Thus they erode in filicide,
Decaying in a state of doubt.
They serve no purpose to the tide,
And so it rubs man's errors out.

Upstream, old boats are splayed out bare.
The distant tide attenuates;
It waxes at uneven rates
And wanes like wheezing bellows air.
Gentle breath on moistened lips.
Now, from the jetty, ghostly men
Look wistfully on ghostly ships.
The industry that built the craft
Was washed away, and, with it, left

The strength to tear them down again.

II

Chatham: Blade Runner
     ironed flat, with
         one crease botched.
The Knicks are missing a Jumbotron;
     It fell behind the bus station.
To the North: Urban decay and history.
To the South: Urban decay and history.
To the East...it is no use. The thing has speakers.
A brief loop details
     local events. It is very brief.

The rain feeds the river;
the river feeds by osmosis.
The pixels fizzle out;
     They are replaced by the industrious.
     The industrious fizzle out;
         they are replaced.
All the while the river scythes
     away at its foundation. The meandering lasso
         will creep and tip it over, the sleeping cow
           lowing as it falls.

III

What is the nature of things?
To minnows, water is as air.
To us, time is as void.

We are not born to padlocked rooms,
Marooned in crystal bowls,
But barracudas shot from wombs;
Transmigrating souls
Piped like data, loath to freeze;
A superfluid ooze,
Like sap suck-siphoned up through trees,
Sluicing through yew tubes.
Thus our waters carry us;
They bear our charge like wires
Past artificial barriers,
Pulsed like flashing fires.
Down silver Tay, down iron Tyne,
Down copper-watered Tiber,
We flicker-thread our crystalline
Internal optic fibre.
We know there is a terminus,
But no-one tells us where it is;
And so we slip inside it, blind
And at a constant speed.
The drag that blocks our leaway lead
Is matched with force behind.
We ebb and flow in pleasure;
We fall into our fall.
An omnipresent pressure makes no pressure felt at all.
For who is moving, and through what?
How splits the light and prism?
All we know's that-which-is-not,
An endless catechism.
Time is distance; distance, time,
And subject to their course are we.

Down their streams all rivers climb,
To join the heavens of the sea.

Now He Is Both Sun And Moon

Now he is both sun and moon,
Just as he was on Earth, for death
Has put no stint upon him.
The Celestial Sphere
Becomes his mighty Globe.

He beholds, with weary eyes,
His great works laid to waste.
He watches Bowdler Bowdlerise,
And Cibber cut and paste.
The Montagues and Capulets,
In Bernstein's West Side Schlock,
Are swapped for greasy Sharks and Jets;
Verona for The Block.
He sees his Avon grave, and gawps
As Foucault, Baudrillard,
Deleuze and Barthes dig up his corpse
To crow, "Who crowned *you* "Bard"?"
And which is worse? To face attack
While dead in Poets' Corner?
Or have your verse, behind your back,
Adapted by Time-Warner?

He seeps into our waking life;
His Shylock, our Exchequer -
A pound of flesh fresh off his knife,
The greedy little fecker.
Richard's twisted Yorkish bones
Are rudely resurrected
To join the staff of Falstaff clones
We Commoners elected.
They seek the skill he once displayed -
To bend, without remorse,
And make the shady backhand trade:
Our kingdom, for a horse.

Now, Stratford is, to his regret,
A glorified bordello.
A Female Woman, Juliet!
An Actual Black Othello!
He scarce believes the sounds they hear;
His face is wracked with smiles,
And, like a Fool, he laughs at Lear,
While rolling in the aisles.
He claps a hand on Marlowe's back;
He finds the scene absurd.
"They didn't change the script, Kit!
They didn't change a word!"

Akira Kurosawa nods -
The cameraman records.
Fifty archers' arrows miss Mifune by a whisker;
Will, rising to his feet, applauds.

Polestar Streetlight

Pitchblack hawthorn subway line
Twigs twist stiff beside me
Antiperson serpentine
Polestar streetlight guide me

Shadows wind at angled speed
Set on fences skimming
Black on black, blacked out they bleed
Flit like lit flight, dimming
Cobbled rootstroke stick my feet
Hid ahead my rest
Where lacks light too lacks there heat
Draw me to thy breast

Make I light of milestone stiles
Languish, shaded, shielded
Bright your shining eye beguiles
Where the hedgerows yielded
Sky and earth penumbra both
Sidewise, I recurse
In pinhole camera undergrowth
Eclipsing in inverse

Polestar streetlight beest my aim
By thy glow beseeken
Take me backways whence I came
Shown home by your beacon
By your beckon, back, migrate
The Everyroad that leads to Rome
Down thy well I gravitate;
Polestar streetlight, guide me home.

Escalatorcleansers

"I have made a discovery which will ensure the supremacy of German music for the next hundred years!"

- Arnold Schoenberg, Vienna, 1921

ARE YE READY, KIDS? (Aye aye, Cap'n!)
HOLD UP YOUR FINGERS!

I.   IMPERATOR CAESAR DIVI FILIVS AVGVSTVS!
II.   TIBERIVS CAESAR DIVI AVGVSTI FILIVS AVGVSTVS!
III.   GAIVS IVLIVS CAESAR AVGVSTVS GERMANICVS!
IV.   TIBERIUS CLAUDIUS CAESAR AUGUSTUS
GERMANICUS!
V.   NERO CLAVDIVS CAESAR AVGVSTVS GERMANICVS

Work smarter, not harder. Exemplified
By today's missed photo.
Two men, a sign -
        "CLEANING IN PROGRESS" -
And an ingenious device.

The men at ground stay level and hold;
The escalator cleans itself
Against
      The Escalatorcleanser.

History is trickery.
Its vestments, sleek and sinuous,
Mask zoetropey-flickery,
Pretending it's continuous.
The needle scoops the record's groove
And gouges out its lint.
The matrix sits, the papers move,
Subjected to a print.
So it is with death and age,
Lost memory and illness.
Fired with ire, we jape and rage
Against unfeeling stillness,
But we forget that we forget,
And ripple on our pond.
We edit out our earthly debt,
Obliviously conned.

But look! A fresh contender.
Some chummy commie Candyman,
Self-styled as our defender.
A quasi-Ozymandian,
Who fobs off for another day
Great promises unkept.
They think they sweep the dirt away,
But they're the dirt that's swept.
They rouse a crowd to scratch a scab

And wade in, locked and loaded,
To chip some diktats on a slab
For time to leave eroded.

History is figureless
When viewed at deepest root.
There, Neros and Caligulas
Receive Time's little boot.
Dictators pass like odours, leached
Like stinking grim cadenzas,
Dimming into codas, bleached
By Escalatorcleansers.

History is slippery,
Its acts a sordid joke.
All is but a frippery;
Revolt must risk revoke.
So fight to give the hungry food,
Fight for your release,
But do not ever self-delude
Your change bring lasting peace.
Escalatorcleanser.
Cleaning in progress.

"Music"

I Do Not Particularly Care For Bands, See

I do not know what bands are for,
Except as proofs of Sturgeon's law:
That every sphere of human wit
Is 95% pure shit.

Bands aren't art;
They want to belong.
Bands are a fossilised chord chart,
But a chord chart's not a song.
Bands hold no surprises;
They're frozen rehearsal.
Bands are sets of compromises;
Creative misdispersal.
Bands are the irrelevant
Names of pricks in lights.
Bands are collected sediment;
Harmonic stalagmites.
A band's a JCB,
Ploughed into the verge
Of a narrow country lane.

They whistle jauntily
And with each crash rehash their dirge
Again and again and again.
Bands are the scams
Of self-deluded scammers
With self-deluded plans,
Preening for the cameras.
Bands are Banksy hanging
The same old mouldy balls.
Bands are drab headbanging
On slowly clapping walls.
A band will take two points,
Trudge the shortest distance,
And purge of any novel joints
The path of least resistance.
A band will class as treachery
The wisdom of a school
Then strive for mystic alchemy
With dust and sand and gruel.
Bands inspect their hairy palms,
Surprised at what they see there,
Then feign excuse with open arms;
"I guess you had to be there."
Each dullard of a band believes
Their thoughts their treasured guests,
Their "influences" on their sleeves
And shirts and shoes and vests.
Bands are nests of Borgias
In grim stylistic ghettos.
Bands are master forgers
Who think they're Canalettos.

Bands are the natural selections
Of humdrum social pressures.
Bands are the rejections
Of any novel measures.
Bands are awful, half-full glasses,
Topped up from their members' arses.
Grey waste; flat land;
That's a band.

This is why I always hated Oasis;
They lowered the stakes of the game.
Everybody's energy sounds different,
But everyone's inertia sounds the same.

Mr Music Man

Who's the smartest of artists?
Who's the smartest of arses?
The cheeriest of chartists,
It's Mr Music Man.
With chipperest of cheek,
For to be careerist,
His notions are the queerest -
His queerest notion being that his notions are unique.

He gruffly masturbates,
Recycling the greats
In solitary vomitary fun.
He'll piously implore
"It's all been done before",
But doesn't understand why it's been done.

The lay he glibly grifts
Predictably uplifts
In ways that make me sad to be alive.
He earnestly emotes
"We only have twelve notes!"
Then writes while only ever using five.

Play your solo shows,
Brave little trooper.
Use your stupid looper,
Off it goes.
Regurgitate your sound.
Great, great. Jeez.
Even a child of eight knows
Locking in keys
Is the wrong way round.
Watch time pass with a flat beat ticking.
Think you're kicking ass but your ass needs kicking.

Disdainfully disclaiming
The notion he's renaming
Old produce for an unobservant eye.
The classic chords all bore ya,
But it's the chordal order
That separates the classics and McFly.

Show me what you got.
Show me what you got.
I'm waiting.
I'm waiting.
You do not hit the spot.
The looper carries on.
The looper carries on.
A busted carillon.
Listen to it go.

Like a broken record.
Like a broken record.
Like a broken record,
Or one that should be so.

Drone

Your music decorates time
Like aerosols on walls.
You sit, job done,
With paint-caked hands.
I, at a distance,
Remain untouched.

High-Pass Filter

If your sound gets out of kilter,
Grab yourself a high-pass filter.
It's the nads.
If you echo around like a dirty dub
In a cavern instead of the Cavern Club,
High-pass filter, lads.
If your vocal channel sticks
Out five feet above the mix,
Your low mids boom and bleed
And your plosives pop like kicks,
Then what you need
Is a high-pass filter.

If it clags like sludge
Or clumping blood,
Or a layer of fudge
On Mississippi mud,
Get a grip, bud;
Take a tip, friend:
Clean your bottom end
With a high-pass filter.

If pervasive bass obscures your hooks

And it sounds as brown as a Rembrandt looks,
If your broth gets spoiled by many cooks -
High-pass filter.
If you're tired of tweaking narrow bands
And it lays as low as the Netherlands
Or some other pancake nation,
You need high-pass filtration.

Keep a little trace of space reserved for bass and beat;
Your frequencies are sequences that do not bear repeat.
So if your lows are fully clogged,
Like wheezing horses being flogged,
High-pass YOU KNOW IT BY NOW.
If your track's way bassy
And you want it to be tasty,
Make your top end spacious;
Crisp and efficacious;
Pure as snow on glaciers;
Get a most bodacious
High-pass filter.

High-pass filter -
Stick it in your chain.
High-pass filter -
Go relax your brain.
High-pass filter, that's the shit.
All your bass belong to it.

Aesthetics

Bait and Switch

Bait and switch
Bait and switch
Low-fat hi-carb protein rich
Theme and development, which one's which
Hit me up punk with the bait and switch

Feed me Seymour with your grand designs
Straight from the mouths of your masterminds
Fall face-first in the drainage ditch
Kindly provided by the bait and switch
Fingers creeping up your neck then pinch
Gently wedgied by a David Lynch
Don't go whining like a basic bitch,
Cuff upside me with a bait and switch

Bait and switch is a shock assault
Knocks down barriers that ain't your fault
Makes all the efforts that you won't expend,
BAM! Y'got bait-and-switched, my friend.
Gated logic, and/or/if

Signposts pointing off a windy cliff
Start with the end then you work it back
Pass you coming up the forward track

La la tralalala la la la
OK good so good so far
La la tralalala la *DA DA*
What? It's a bait and switch? Oh. AAARGH!
Struck like cattle eyes wide with trust
Stung with a stun gun, biting dust
You got scratched on an unknown itch
Someone hit you with a bait and switch

Malkovich Malkovich Mal-ko-vich
Malkovich Malkovich Mal-ko-vich
Malkovich Malkovich Mal-ko-vich
What? John Cusack? Bait and switch!

Points were made but they came too late
You got goosed and it wiped your slate
What you thought was gonna come now ain't
Feed line, punchline, flatline, faint.
Popped to the top of your top pop picks,
When you see it, you'll shit bricks
Fell for the spell of the same lame tricks
Switched-out bait is how I get my kicks.

Heavens defend me from the evil twin
Who let slip feelings I was keeping in
He names names and then he calls them out
For only writing what they write about

Specified and everybody groans and knows
There ain't no game but the plain plain prose
What got read was a dead straight pitch
The bait's on a plate and there ain't no switch
Ain't no switch.
Ain't no bait.
I might have listened but you came too late.

Sounds About Right

You write a lot of pieces
That have no central thesis
No flow and all staccato
Hip-hyperkinesis
No beat and all rubato
Insistent, abstract, ceaseless,
All cheese and no tomato
On micron-thin-sliced pizzas.
Floppy rubber beaters
Slap absent silent drums, in
Elasticated meters
Through bland continuums,
Atop a coy continuo,
Implicit but forgot,
Displaying what you do not know
To others who do not.

Open your mind, open your mind
Sounds about right
What will you find, what will you find
Sounds about right

Who cares if Leibniz got there first,

For who the heck is he?
Who's to say which version's worst?
Please treat each equally.
You'd know, if you'd read Derrida,
The message is the text,
But no, for you dread Derrida.
No YouTube channel? NEXT.
Each intellectual challenger's
Philosopher anathema.
You pruned your reading list
To fill the mic-lead catheter
With what your betters pissed.

The revolution's already begun
Sounds about right, sounds about right
We are all one, we are all one
Sounds about right, sounds about right

The universe is mystic myth
Brim-full of phoney Buddhas
Who speak of it like Jaden Smith;
Rhetorical do-gooders
Who say that true reality
Is out of human reach
For all is non-duality,
Then prove their facts with speech.
Glutamate and little meat,
Is what I'd call your prose.
Pray sit a silent year's retreat,
Then tell me how that goes.

When will we open our minds to concepts beyond our understanding?
When will we rise against the putrid, perverted, evil, greedy bankers and politicians
And shoot in the face each one who does not realise
That we are all the same beautiful children of God?

It's Impossible To Learn To Plow By Reading Books

        You can
Learn to sew for penguins from a pamphlet,
        Or
Crochet crêpe cravates for crows or rooks
        Or
Knit a shirt that fits a fossa
But you'll find that it's impossi-
        -ble to learn to plow by reading books

        There are
People who will sell you
        Learned
Tomes but I must tell you
        That the
People who will sell you them are crooks.
        The
Learning is exacting,
        You must
Learn by re-enacting.
        It's im -
- possible to learn to plough from books

You
Cannot learn to plow by reading books.
It's impossi -
- ble to learn to plow by reading books.
The
Other agriculturalists will give you filthy looks,
If you
Try to learn to plow by reading books.

Your
Fellow farming students
Will ac -
- cuse you of imprudence, and
Anyone with half a brain expects
There's no
Value in a thesis
Or its
Lucid exegesis,
For you
Cannot learn to plow by reading texts

The
Learning is slow-going;
First you
Work your way from hoeing
Up to
Tethering your chisel to your mule
Then you
Practise yoking oxen
Navi -
- gate a fields with rocks in

And they
Use no printed notes in ploughing school

You will
Have to leave the library,
De -
- scend your tower of ivory
And
Purge your mind of Balzac, Blake, bell hooks,
Beryl
Bainbridge, Billy Burroughs,
They won't
Help you harrow furrows,
It's not
Possible to learn to plough from books

There are
Books on every topic
Bursting
Forward, phototropic;
For
Any skill they'll share the why and how
But
Sometimes that's too narrow;
Drop the
Book, pick up your farrow,
It's im -
- possible,
From books,
to learn
to plough.

Balance

I know the price of everything
And the value of nothing,
For value is like hot gold dust cakes these days,
There ain't much of it about.
What's worthwhile now? Iunno.
No filtration's done.
Every day's a talent show
And every round's round one.
It sets its stock before me
To bore me with the tawdry.

Sat in centres for the arts
Paying my respects
To mulched-up bundled half-dead parts
Of musical effects.
Put in efforts, get back nils
On sinusoidal slides.
Push my go-cart up steep hills
Which have no other sides.
Films filled with spiteful silence,
Or words that work out wrong,
Can take their talk and hie hence;
Two hours is hours too long.
The classics are no fun;
I've had enough of Beethoven
I cannot hear his Fifth again
I am *DONE DONE DONE DOOOONE*

Live life like a boring man,
Thoroughly self-taught.
Play like a Victorian
Who plays because they ought.
Like my mother, bless her,
Freed from her young,
Who spent her spare time ringing bells
Because they would not ring themselves
And needed to be rung.

Books!
Books whose titles, as a lad,
Would lodge inside my brain,
Destined not to die,
Then taunt and haunt in faint refrain,
Dug over in The Grauniad,
Though Christ alone knows why.
Quickly picked but slowly read;
Stultifying mess,
Which says what Holby City said
In half an hour or less.
Press-ganged by a Kitchener
With qualitative lies.
I often pity literature
Has no IgNobel prize,
Just gin without the fizz.
I cannot fathom what they meant;
It either isn't excellent,
Or won't say why it is.

Entertain me, world;
I am tired.
Place your great works in a queue
And wheel them past my eyes.
We shall see if that will do;
If it satisfies.
Waste my time constructively;
Bear what fun occurs.
Treat my time reductively;
Fill the empty years.
Do as you would be done to;
Sort the coarse from fine.
Shouldn't someone else have done so
Somewhere down the line?

Tell Me The Truth About Art

Oil is slippery and feeds the wealthy;
Pigment will flatter you then stain your hands.
I trust neither.

The paintings that last from the centuries past
Were building on works of their time,
Which built on the Greeks and such other antiques,
Their myths and their reason and rhyme.
But I am no Greek and my knowledge is weak;
When I'm stood in a room with a view,
I huff and blush lest I not know which is best.
Sir, what should a stupid boy do?
I find unfantastic the classics in aspic,
And view them with dubious duty.
My reverence fades as their references age;
What shall we do, what shall we do, with
        All this youthless beauty?
Now Sewell is dead, who will stick in my craw?
I doubt like the greatest Descartes.
I think that I think, but I'm sure I'm not sure;
Tell me the truth about art.

Who will step forward to challenge me next?

Who will allay my concern?
I gaze, out of phase with academies' texts.
Who else will teach me to learn?
The Fauvists are beasts and the Stuckists are stuck;
The others are cliques and elites,
And judgement by time yields to judgement by luck,
Or judgement by likes and retweets.

I open the door and I wonder, what is it,
This scant pile of shite on the floor?
It's minimalism, but isn't exquisite,
So how should I know what it's for?
Cases of curios, lain in arrays,
The fruit of a clever chrome clone
From Goldsmith's, if that's where they go to these days,
Or some school too cool to be known.
A sleek preening genius, stuck up by boards,
Who conquers but stoops to have fun;
Off galivanting and winning awards
That seemingly need to be won.
Supposing it's Emperor's clothing, self-loathing
Returns me to ignorant times.
My philistinism on minimalism
And other egregious crimes
Was fear of not knowing where culture was going
And was I about to be conned?
For, as with all scenes I recall from my teens,
It's dredged up by memory's wand,
An endless chaconne that repeats on and on,
So in Rothko's Chapel I kneel
And pray to repent of the type of resent

That I felt but now long to repeal.
So how to decide what to praise or deride,
When I bow to the PoMo conceit
That the modernist dream was a problem, their scheme
Just a sketch of its selfsame defeat?
And if Sturgeon was right and in twenty of each
Nineteen are cack-handed or fluff,
And if four out of five are pitched out of my reach,
Well, a hundred is barely enough.

But
Every so often I visit a space
That my memory falsely recalls,
As if someone better had taken my taste
And laid it with love on the walls,
Curating by anticipating my need,
As if it had split from my heart.
They patched up my gashes before they could bleed,
And told me the truth about art.

People

David Foster Wallace

David Foster Wallace
King of the wild frontier
David Foster Wallace
He of the logorrhoea

He rides the wide savannah
In a star-spangled bandanna
To analyse the people of the Veldt
His style is dense and graphic
And stiltedly empathic,
If empathy were something thought not felt

David Foster Wallace
King of the MFA-s
David Foster Wallace
Footnotes droning on for days

He reads your mind like Yoda
Then writes it like a coder
With programmer grammar in interwoven threads
As if some Grecian chorus

Had swallowed a thesaurus
Then printed out the contents of their heads

David Foster Wallace
He of the tennis socks
David Foster Wallace
Something of a Joyce for Jocks

He shows off all his know-how
By mixing high- and low-brow
At all times, to the limit of his strength
He doesn't go and wreck it
By getting too Sam Beckett
But heck it if he doesn't try with length

David Foster Wallace
King of the modern lit
David Foster Wallace
Franzen, but less shit

So if you think that Pynchon
Deserves a pitchfork lynchin'
For making books impersonal and queer
Let Wallace fix that schism
With post-postmodernism
It lets you jerk around but stay sincere

David Foster Wallace
Best of the best by far
David Foster Wallace
(Notwithstanding Mary Karr)

(Sotto voce)
Weights of expectation
And wasted medication
Drained out David's reasons to exist
Tired of lily-gilding
He leapt his burning building.
David Foster Wallace, you'll be missed.

David Foster Wallace,
You were A Supposedly Fun Thing.
David Foster Wallace
Ride into the sunset, Pale King.

Poor Leonard Cohen

Poor old Leonard Cohen
Become a broken heart
Made himself unhappy
To make unhappy art
Beauties came and beauties went
Testing Leonard's strength
Every lover heaven sent
Kept he at arm's length
Never then would Leonard yield
Safe behind his curtain
Lest his pleasure showed.
Leonard, rest your staff and shield
Life will take that burden
And give you back its load.

Daliland

Daliland's a far far land,
A La-La-Land Gondwanaland
Of mountain lakes become unfixed,
Of flats and crags and creeks and drought
And skies and waters intermixed
And sundry tundras strewn about
With whatsoever sprang to mind
Thought worthy to be left behind.

The sands' expanses, coloured dusts,
Display, like faded palimpsests,
Platonic or distended breasts,
The subjects of abstracted lusts.
They hang around in scenes comprised
Of virgins propped on balconies
Who end up auto-sodomised
By virtue of their chastities.
Swans and Ledas, limply posed
For congress coyly hinted at;
Their gazes blank and indisposed;
The stage, like their expressions, flat.
Clay-faced Autumn Cannibals
Consume, as mute as animals,

Themselves, in Onanistic kisses;
Salvador becomes Narcissus.

All is housed in ill-fit skins,
So, if a second form appends,
The way the former form begins
Need not determine how it ends.
All warmth is cold, all fire is pale,
All light the child of shade.
All size discorrellates to scale;
All colours run to fade.
All is lax, equanimous,
A futile neutral scene;
The hellfires of Hieronymous,
Spread thin as margarine.
A branch split from our mortal coil;
A country far from civil war,
Where nothing bears the fruits of toil
And nothing merits fighting for,
For if this *this* looks like this *that*,
Or if that *that* looks like this *this*,
It be but games of tit-for-tat;
There is no missing link to miss.
A land devoid of consequence
Reshot behind a tilt-shift lens,
Refilled with antiseptic sense
By hands that only seek to cleanse.

So suchlike hangs within the Tate,
The Prado, Louvre, the Hermitage,
And punters flock to venerate;

To marvel at the strange ménage
Of twisted siblings frame by frame,
A context out of context, each
Bereft of use and void of aim
As watches bent upon a beach.

Richard Dawkins Eve

Ring the bell,
Knock at the door,
Turn around and leave.
Silent night,
Secular night,
Richard Dawkins Eve.

Dress in slacks and brogues and tweed
And what the living don,
Then do not ring. There is no need.
Carry slowly on.
It doesn't matter what, as long
As people disbelieve;
Denial macht us right and strong,
On Richard Dawkins Eve.

Go tell the sons of Abraham
Their efforts went to waste
And time will mark their faith a sham,
Anointing them disgraced.
Bentham's light will shine the way,
Converting the naive
In prelude to All Dawkins Day;

Richard Dawkins Eve.

Give thanks you have no soul to lose,
For fate is saved from chance,
And bless beloved Dawkipoos
With praise and funding grants.
Vampire bats flit all about,
Fit subjects for dissection,
And if their bite begets you doubt,
It be but an infection.
We reverence the skeleta
And what they represent -
The breedings of millennia;
We grovel, reverent.
White labcoats disappose white sheets
To paddle in faith's shallows
As Darwin's ghost bestrides the streets
In Atheist All-Hallows
And all such dead souls represent
No thing that one might grieve,
Nor mourn its passing, nor repent,
On Richard Dawkins Eve.

The science-fear be not the fear
That all might be destroyed,
But knowing all that be be here,
And death is but the void.
Thou never shalt rejoin thy kith,
Nor readjoin thy roots,
For life eternal be a myth -
Go quake amid thy boots.

We turn our backs upon the doors,
Open up our tupperware,
Unwrap our pre-bought candy bar,
Take bites, then find some folks to scare
Describing Mother Nature's laws
Exactly as they are.

The Best The West Could Give To You Has Gone *(Letter to Ashraf Fayadh)*

[In 2016, Phil Kane asked that Medway poets write or perform works in support of Ashraf Fayadh, a Palestinian poet imprisoned in Saudi Arabia on trumped up charges of apostasy. I tried writing something appropriate, but couldn't stop thinking about another event of that time, the death of David Bowie. This is the result.]

Wild is the Wind
Outside.
Ashes to Ashes,
Quicksand.
Scary Monsters and Super Creeps.

Everyone Says Hi.
Hallo Spaceboy,
Future Legend.
Little Wonder;
You Belong In Rock and Roll.
All The Young Dudes,
Heroes.

Watch That Man.
Sound and Vision. Fame.

What's Really Happening?
Time.
Five Years -
Golden Years,
Because You're Young.

Under Pressure.
Jump They Say -
The Last Thing You Should Do.
This is not America.
Hang On To Yourself.

Where Are We Now?
We Are The Dead.

You want apostates?
Well apostates we got
But we just went and lost ourselves
The greatest of the lot.

Mary Berry

Why you gotta bake
Why you gotta bake
Why you gotta bake bake bake that cake
Why you gotta bake
Why you gotta bake
Mary Mary Berry? Now
I don't trust no thin woman,
Prickly like a pin cushion,
Kinda skinny looking
Who don't eat her own cooking.
All else is forsaken
For the sake of baking,
But does it slake the aching?
Mary Mary Berry.
Does it soothe your little soul,
Bridge the troubled water,
Perfecting your profiterole and
Schwarzwälder Kirschtorte? Now,

I don't mean to be
        rude, dude,
But what didya do with the
        food food?

I'd be shocked if
      you'd chewed
Half the pastries
      you'd accrued.
Maybe maybe Mary Berry
Got herself a fancy man she
Stuffs with panettone,
Angel cake and frangipane so
He won't leave her lonely,
For if he has enough to scoff
He'll blossom by inflation,
And never up and wander off,
Kept chained by gravitation.
But still. Still, that's
      still a lot of cake.
Still a lot of cake for her to bake.
Maybe she's got little cliques
Of cake-addicted feeding freaks.
Who think they get a cushy deal
By being Mary's fella
But then she slams the shutter screen
And lets the little piggies squeal,
Locked inside her cellar,
Siphoned full of buttercream.
Swelling into fleshy spheres
With little log-like legs
Their cries are silent; Mary's ears
Attend the cracks of eggs.
She's got money and time to kill;
She's got a pit like Buffalo Bill.
She's got sponge with toffee gunge on

She's got gimps to fatten
She's got threads and a sewing pattern
Pinned up by her dungeon.
"It rubs the lotion on its skin,
It takes the cake and shoves it in"
And while they shriek for sweet release
She keeps them locked below
And puffs them up like foie gras geese;
"Grow, my pretties...grow".
And grow her little pretties shall;
They eat until they ache.
Mary is a busy gal -
She's got cakes to bake.

Finlay Veiled-Proxy

Who's that in the limo, pulling up in Leicester Square,
Smiling for the cameras at the glitzy premiere,
Ready to be featured in tomorrow's magazine?
It's Finlay Veiled-Proxy, the tsar of stage and screen.

The blandest of the superstars, a wolf without the teeth,
Like crayon lain upon a vase, he masks the glass beneath.
The darling of the writer, the actor's favoured muse;
He sparks up like a lighter in whichever way you choose.

People call up Finlay when they want their lives rewritten
In ways by which their paramours might plausibly be smitten.
Ring up David Tennant, send an email to Matt Smith;
Finlay is the polish on the man behind the myth.

Finlay is hermaphrodite; the feminine auteur
Would ring up Finlay if they might bestow a part on her.
Finlay moulds to any race; what Finlay likes the best
Is moulding to the face of someone beaten and oppressed.
Finlay fits all genders. His ambit is complete:
Emmerdale, EastEnders. Coronation Street.
A charlatan, a liar, a jobsworth substitute,
Looking like his owner, only better, younger, cute.

If you need some schmuck to spell out what you represent,
Finlay is the man to tell the public what you meant.
He will fill your manifest with what you might have said,
So if you cannot be the best, use Finlay in your stead.

The fount from which artist draws;
Finlay Veiled-Proxy.
The portrait, but without the flaws;
Finlay Veiled-Proxy.
The author's twitching unborn twin,
Their Texas Chainsaw second skin,
A doppelganging next-of-kin -
Finlay Veiled-Proxy.

If your screenplay needs confess the torments of your soul,
Then settle not for any less; let Finlay be your whole.
He'll be a magic mirror, filled with everything you do:
Finlay Veiled-Proxy - the living spit of you.

Georgia O'Keefe

Georgia O'Keefe
Georgia O'Keefe
She painted flowers that looked like ladies viewed from beneath
The archetypal artists were agog and appalled;
"We must insist pudenda be close-legged and bald!
We're complaining to the censor-in-chief,
Mzz Georgia O'Keefe!"

Georgia O'Keefe,
Georgia O'Keefe,
They looked like Venus flytraps only minus the teeth.
They flowed into the canvas like the seeping of ink,
They came in many colours, only some of them pink.
Buckling the shackle of the patriarchal manacle,
Both plausibly botanical and quasi-anatomical.
It's only a yoni, or is that a leaf?
Whichever; you're phenomenal,
Mzz Georgia O'Keefe

Places

The Pentagram Centre

Sat squat vacant lot
Fifteen stories high
A several-level who-knows-what
Where money went to die
A long con gone wrong
Abandon hope, who enter
This concrete Necronomicon
The Pentagram Centre

Blank dead square feet
The fruit of evil deed
Where nobody may seek retreat
Though many be in need
Take ye flight or take ye care
Kneel o ye repenter
A craftless loveless Lovecraft lair
The Pentagram Centre

Cerberi are kept in check
Near automatic doors
By men with barbed ink round their neck

Who live beyond our laws.
The guardsman of the seeping bricks,
His face a strained magenta,
Admits you. Past his River Styx,
The Pentagram Centre.

So it sits there. Aged, depraved,
The inverse of invention.
It's said the road to Medway's paved
With puke and good intention.
Who laid down its dour design?
Who was the inventor
Who set in stone this Frankenstein,
The Pentagram Centre?

Critics bitch and critics chide
And call my words unfair,
For truth and beauty lie inside -
But half its floors lie bare.
Will it ever be redeemed,
Freed from its indenture
To be the land of which we dreamed?
The Pentagram Centre.

People Dump

Here is imbalance, Koyaanisqatsi.
A mismatched ratio;
People, without
The things that people do.
Indistinguished storage bays,
No sign that they are left.
Roads freed from destinations,
Or the responsibilities of width;
Long views clear of pedestrians.
Somehow the infected land
Grew this thing,
Cheap property upon cheap property.
Mitosis by exponents.

Minimally stocked shops;
The local notice board a stopped clock.
A doctor, a builder,
Flapping their hands at the march of time.
Older younger sibling schools,
Buried in the back streets;
I hope they teach geography,
Economics.

What is it like at night?
I will never have grounds to find out.
Calm like the woods, I would guess,
Only stiller. Street lights beat down the noise
And drown out the stars.

Its bulk obscures its exits;
All one sees is fields,
A green belt notched too tight
Around a fresh Fresh Kills.
Leave by the blue moon bus,
If you've time to wait;
You will.

Boulevards

I want to run to places I can run
From side to side between the traffic,
Pavements more distant
Than Leicester Square and Covent Garden.
Office-flanked canyons,
Buildings of uncertain purpose,
Logos blurred in haze;
England has none of this.
I miss it. I long for Barcelona,
Not for the Sagrada Familia
Or the gauche, dead Parque Guell,
Where Gaudí preens, the cracked-tile peacock,
But for its exits and entrances
When gates once kept out Visigoths,
Presumably. Now, gentle risings
Deepen its pooled architecture.
Its trench ingressed, my gaze
Guides ever upward. Far from drowned,
I join the skies.

The Antisocial Club

The antisocial club.
Where antisocial thinkers
Are antisocial drinkers;
My go-to type of pub.

The antisocial club;
Wherein the expectation
Is whistles being whet
In sodden isolation,
Gazes unmet.
Guard yourself from prying ears,
Shielded by screens.
Choose from some sundry beers
In vending machines
Or brave the barman. He is trained,
Stray from your seat.
His banter, sparse. Self-restrained,
Tasteful, discreet.
"Whatcha drinking, sir? Do tell.
Shh! Don't be crass.
Order via ASL,
Point with your glass.
By pantomime and déjà vu

Your round is quietly bought.
We know to serve up less than two,
But greater than nought.
Total up our second guess;
Sir will now pay.
Of course we can do contactless,
We contact less each day."

Steal between the stools.
Find a shady table,
Spill a little bottled beer,
Pick its paper label
And peel it into pools.
Sit in isobooths,
Slowly disappear.
Plug headphones into dead phones,
Contemplate grim truths.
No-one ever checks us.
Each one-man hub
A solitary nexus,
An antisocial club.

Gravesend

This Poem Is Not About Gravesend

You don't turn up at arseholes' wakes
Clad in gay apparels
You let men grieve, for goodness sakes;
You don't shoot fish in barrels.
You do not kerb-stomp men with clogs -
Their shoes are their affair.
You don't kick dying underdogs;
Reader, have a care.
Don't be a bottom-feeder, dude,
Feasting on decay;
It's inappropriate and rude;
You profit, others pay.
You do not act like victimhood's
A set result of fate.
You do not overlook the goods,
As if time ran too late.
You do not sit apart and judge,
Pouting, both arms crossed.
The truth is often much too much;
Don't crow at what got lost. Don't

Roll your eyes at specks in eyes
When planks are in your own.
You do not need to patronise
Where one may not condone.

This is a problem.
How do we point out a problem
Without pointing out the symptoms?
Without symptoms, there is no problem -
But the symptoms are not the problem.

Some go supercritical
When faced with life gone wrong
And feed their muse a bitter pill
Through verse or stage or song.
They blame the patsy for the act
That men, subjectified,
Were forced, unwilling, to enact
By those who bought their pride.
So don't confuse the cause and means;
The message and the code;
The scripts and the resulting scenes;
The reading and the ode.
Find fault with the universe,
As if that's what it's for,
And flag yourself as something worse -
A sign and nothing more.
No-one likes a wag who points
At what is deemed a sin,
Stripped of sinew, bones and joints -
A custard in a skin.

So when I stand, unbudging,
Begrudging others' fun,
It seems that I judge judging -
And thus, I guess, I'm done.

Kabaddi

*Kabaddi kabaddi kabaddi kabaddi kabaddi kabaddi kabaddi
kabaddi*
Kabaddi kabaddi kabaddi kabaddi kabaddi kabaddi kabaddi

It isn't like golf 'cause you don't need a caddy
Kabaddi kabaddi kabaddi kabaddi kabaddi kabaddi kabaddi

It's played by both sexes but seems mostly laddy
Kabaddi kabaddi kabaddi kabaddi kabaddi kabaddi kabaddi

I cannot make out who's the goodie or baddie
Kabaddi kabaddi kabaddi kabaddi kabaddi kabaddi kabaddi

When somebody scores, they shout "WHO'S THE DADDY?"
Kabaddi kabaddi kabaddi kabaddi kabaddi kabaddi kabaddi

They used to show it on Channel 4
But it ain't on Channel 4 no more
'Cause Channel 4 are faddy
Kabaddi kabaddi kabaddi kabaddi kabaddi kabaddi kabaddi

The pitch is bare and rarely clogged
Except for when it's waterlogged

Like some kind of rice paddy
Kabaddi kabaddi kabaddi kabaddi kabaddi kabaddi kabaddi

The title is Tamil, the same in Punjabi
The players are sometimes surprisingly flabby
They never stop chanting, you've got to be gabby
They play it in Delhi but not Abu Dhabi
Kabaddi kabaddi kabaddi kabaddi kabaddi kabaddi kabaddi

People seem to love it madly;
I would like to too, but, sadly,
Understand it rather badly.
Kabaddi kabaddi kabaddi
Kabaddi kabaddi kabaddi
Kabaddi kabaddi kabaddi kabaddi
Kabaddi,
　　　Kabaddi,
　　　　　Kabaddi.

Escape Room

Have you been to the Escape Room,
Escape Room,
Escape Room?
Have you been to the Escape Room
Down Berkeley Crescent way?
In the Georgian-Victorian colonnade
Like a kinda half-run Bath
In the emptied bleached-out beached arcade
Where the road runs a D-shaped path
Down by the old clock tower
Come and let the time tick tock
Spend yourself a pleasant hour,
Just you and a room and a lock.
Wave to the man with the camera
Peeking through the fisheye lens
Bent like the bottom of a jamjar
Looking at your round-faced friends.
They've got a puzzling conundrum
They've got unconnected dots
They've got Gordonian knots to be undone
They've got escapes from the humdrum, son.
Everybody wants to come where
You can be a movie star

Make believe that you're all somewhere -
Anywhere that isn't where you are.

Spin roundabout in your hamster wheel
Your little knock-off Crystal Maze
Turn a tiny problem to a five-course meal
For days and days and days
Dust the place for ultraviolet fingerprints
Fumble with your Rubik's cubes
Beg the kindly cameraman to drop some hints
Squeal like a bunch of noobs
      Then
Visit the other escape room
Escape room
Escape room
Visit the other escape room
Come and take a seat, sit down
And wait for a friendly high-speed train
To whisk you out of town

Sadness

Passionate Man

I longed to be a passionate man
With all my beating heart
I mapped what progress progress can
All plotted on my careworn chart
I sought out such best algebras
As intersect with human wit
Then spent my time in error bars
To try lines of best fit

For every evening misbegun
Crash-landed at its own defeat
I worked out what I should have done
Within that moment's instant heat
So if said circumstance, exact,
Should fall, recursive, unto me,
I'd know how, next time, to react
With practised spontaneity.

By sines of life we rollercoast,
Arisen from the ashen,
Then dash down through this earthly host;
All come to nought, this passion.

She Liked It When I Fought

She liked it when I fought
When I got overwrought
Becoming antiandrogyne
To satisfy her honour
By satisfying mine

And, warmly welcomed, once returned,
Although I found my fingers burned,
My ribs beat black and blue,
At least I tried to beat another -
That's what real boys do.

Her axioms were blunt assaults
Which, alternating true and false
According to her mood,
Prepared me for a big wide world
She wildly misconstrued.

Her bestest cure for life's hard knocks
Was quietly fitting in the box
Of thirty years ago.
If such solutions did not work,
What others could she know?

Now when my life is not delight
I find the culprit, then I fight,
And I become the blame.
For I was taught the fighter, foe,
Bully, victim, cause and woe
Are one and all the same.

Playlist Roulette

Music from my ninth year.
My parents fought downstairs;
Here it is, dragged up
Like it were disco.
Paul Simon sings:
"Fat Charlie the Archangel files for divorce."
Too close to home,
Age has not mellowed it.
I didn't ask to feel this way,
Weeping in a public space.

Here lies playlist roulette.
They would show the death of Bambi's mother
On loop, if they could.
Cake the walls in scriptures;
CGI pietàs.

One boy beside me, one across.
Which father am I today,
Weak or repressed?
I already have lunch to deal with.
They are old enough to know
It's OK, or not yet

Old enough to know things.
Explanation's the hard part;
Crippled senseless sadness,
And if I speak, my speech will fail
Before my tears can fill its cracks.
Let it out, eh?
Later, maybe.

Every place is filled with risks;
Rooms and towns and motor cars,
Vessels of profit, bought into the notion
You cannot cheapen what is free.
Speed down the M4;
Turn away, well up.
We're a safety hazard,
Circumstance and me.

They are X-Factor happy to sing.
Burst forth the new harmonies;
Joy to the world, camaraderie.
Hang the sad author,
It's ours now, ours,
In this moment, here.
The passion stripped from every hallelujah;
Breath is for song, of course.
Cold and broken hallelujahs
In a warm room full of love.

Sail on, silver girl,
Any way the wind blows.
Stupid face gone leaky
In the middle of Pizza Hut.

Farmer's Gun

Distant farmer's bullet
Whipcrack of the gun
Wince and count my life down
3 2 1
Head still here. Skull uncracked.
Brain in place and all intact.

Would that it were supersonic
Sudden unexpected death,
Visiting with nonexistence.
Maybe next time, eh?
"Fireworks!" says my youngest,
He laughs, I smile. Maybe one day
I will see stars.

Kill Switch

Hey,
Want to get a pay out?
Apparently, you can.
A way out would be way out,
Man. Way out.
LET ME TELL YOU ALL A BOUT

The kill switch switches
Something unbeknown
The kill switch itches
And won't be left alone
The kill switch crackles
And comes in many shapes
The kill switch cackles
And offers quick escapes
The kill switch stimulates
The parts that you want shut
The kill switch simulates
A total power cut
The kill switch arcs
The kill switch sparks
The kill switch leaves you in infinite darks
The kill switch clamours

And asks that you attend
The kill switch stammers
In ways you cannot mend
The kill switch dares you
And begs you take its heed
The switch outstares you;
L'appel du vide.
The switch tantalises
With something clean and pure
The switch advertises
A magical mystery tour
The kill switch makes you
Pay some self-respects
The kill switch breaks you then it quickly disconnects
The kill switch pokes you
Towards a greater good
The switch provokes you
And won't be understood
The kill switch shorts out
It blows your little fuse
It wipes all thoughts out
And blackens out your blues
The switch
The switch
The switch
The switch
It offers many options only asking of you which
The switch
The switch
It chills you to the bone
And one way or another you will leave the switch,

Alone.

Fluoxetine

Drink a little philtre, keep
Your psyche squeaky clean.
Learn to whistle while you weep,
With fluoxetine.
It drug me in to rope-a-dope,
Plumb tuckered from my lies,
And all it cost was all my hope;
Fluoxetine, fluoxetine, fluoxetine, fluoxetine,
Prozac in disguise.
A mix of wine and radium;
A half-life under glass.
I did not feel arcadian,
But time would rocket past
Like signposts on a motorway
And fall back, unreturned,
Stowing things of note away;
I did not feel concerned.
The outside world went screwball.
I bathed, amidst a haze;
As textured as a cue ball,
As ruffled as green baize,
And faced my reinvention:
A zombie, stripped of soul.

But zombies have intention;
Zombies have a goal.
Day breaks, drained of vim and wrath.
I mumble, as I wake,
"I thought I pulled the covers off...
Oh, sorry - my mistake."
Then rise, besheeted, mummified,
Through soupy neutral air
Which permeates the void inside
In lieu of full repair.
In lieu of full repair.
How, what, when, where, begins my full repair?

My sole memory of that time:
Talking to my doctor,
A beautiful, kind, beautiful black woman doctor,
Thinking in a drift: I can make her happy
By telling her it's working.
Conscious I will never create,
Never love, never meditate,
Never do those things whose lacks
Put me on these pills.

I see you.
I see you.
Fluoxetine, I see you.
I saw, with muffled buffered shock,
The choice I had to face,
Between my anger's crushing rock
And numbness's hard place,
And hid you on the highest shelf.

I braced for what came next,
And stole you down to steel myself
Against your side-effects.
So as I tired of living tithed,
You took a leave of ease
And crept out likeways you arrived:
Between two solstices,
Departing like a lifted mist.
I slowly unimmerse,
And suddenly I re-exist,
For better or for worse.

So now I have an extra ex,
Who forced me to behave,
Then giggled and denied me sex,
Or all the fun it gave.
Fluoxetine, I hope you find
Someone who you can aid;
The welcoming compliant mind
Of someone less afraid.
Our cookie fortune, in the end,
Was not to live as two.
It isn't you, it's me, old friend.
But also -
        IT WAS YOU.

When All You Have Is A Hammer

When all you have is a hammer
Then everyone looks like nails
And everything needs hammering
Even when hammering fails

The doctor learns in doctor school
That evidence is base
And thus adopts a likely tool
Then works it with straight face
For learned tomes were monogrammed
To sell each paradigm
And measured outcomes be they damned
Stop... Hammer time.
So though their pills and therapies
Be old wives' aged tales
They state suchlike as certainties;
The hammer hammers nails.

I, no opaque snowflake prince,
Am common as can be
A white whine straight man bag of hints,
So why can't they fix me?
Allopathy huffed and shrugged

And said, as if to care,
"Perhaps he might be lightly drugged,
Or hugged and told, 'There there'".

We cling unto the talking cure
And keep our feelings dosed,
Or else to live is to endure,
Some skulking, sullen ghost
Without a happy end in sight;
The needs are never met.
We pray with counselling they might,
But have not been so yet.
Harried worried therapists
Bleed heart each time we speak
And manage not to slap our wrists,
Just like they did last week
When last we told our eldest news
In never-ending stammer
For we are loose cross-headed screws
And all they have is a hammer.

Hail Mary, full of grace
Hail Mary, full of grace
Every day in every way
I get a little better.

Nick O'Teen

Perhaps you might share this early memory of mine.
When visiting the doctor, I would sit in a waiting room
Wherein were provided comics and posters.
Superman -
        - his image licensed for the good of public health -
        would battle the villain
                "NICK-O-TEEN",
An anthropomorphised cigarette
Of presumably Irish descent.

Om mane padme hum
Om mane padme hum
Om mane padme hum
Something wicked this way come

Sat on steps
Knees one inch
Above my hips
A makeshift church
Breathe, breathe
Slow, slow
Are we nearly there yet?
No...no.

Careless awareness
Familiar reminders
Snake up spinewise
Same bright shivers
Self-composed and self-estranged
All is the same and all is changed.
Split by subtle boundaries,
Arousal maps out territories.
Sat on one side, ecstasies;
Sat on the other side, horror stories.

Who's that creeping?
Nick O'Teen
Drifting through the kitchen?
Nick O'Teen
Fag butt bent hat brown and singed
Came by to visit when I came unhinged

Smells like loose leaf rolled up shag
Just like Grampa smoked
Stole my baby in a burlap bag
Silenced, poisoned, choked
Two-Face face
Skinless sinew
Slips his stinking sickness in you

Nailscrapes creak round unlocked doors
Glitterball peepholes, *Sh!* don't look
Weeping sepia sandblock claws
Thanks you kindly for the child he took
Scratch your cheek

Taints with stains
Slides through the window but the fear remains

The fault was mine.
Was it? No,
The fault was mine.

Stand steadfast, Siddhartha said
And beest thou recompensed;
I did not know the kinds of dread
I would be set against
So when the thoughts you hide behind
Slip limply to the floor,
Be watchful, for an open mind
Becomes an open door.

Broken Biscuit Assortment

Pyracantha

In the jungle, black as slate,
The pyracantha lays in wait,
Languidly unsheathing claws
To tear into that throat of yours.

In the cortex, something stirs;
The pyracantha hums and whirrs.
Deep within your frontal lobes
Its bundled neurons pulse like strobes.

In the depths, a flickering sheen;
The pyracantha slips unseen.
Living fossil, lithe and thin,
Shimmering its dorsal fin.

In the dungeon, evil dwells;
The pyracantha casts his spells.
Incantating, shifting shape;
Roll D20 to escape.

In some prehistoric age

The pyracantha shrieks with rage,
Hushing but to stuff its maw
With bloody lumps of stegosaur.

I am but a simple man;
All I want's a simple answer.
Riddle this, whoever can:
What the heck's a pyracantha?

Under the Cannabis Tree

Down I laid me in yon field;
Thought me my wounds and troubles healed,
But by the sap my fate was sealed
Under the cannabis tree
Fragrance sharp and sugar sweet
I sank beneath its silken sheet
To suckle at the devil's teat
Under the cannabis tree

Don't eat the fruit of the cannabis tree
Or you'll become its slave
Don't eat the root of the cannabis tree
Unless you seek your grave.
If you sleep by the cannabis tree,
All night hold your breath
Or wail and weep by the cannabis tree;
Its spores are certain death

Do not hark to the cannabis tree
Beware its siren curse
Don't smoke the bark of the cannabis tree
Its bite is far far worse.
Mark ye well its lethal leaf

It taketh deathly tolls
Its catkin reefers run a reef
On which men wreck their souls
And while your mind may phase prostrate
In lazy dozy zen
Your earthly form will copulate
With filthy foreign men

Nothing shall exempt you,
Despite what you believe
The demon tree will tempt you
Like Satan tempted Eve.
So don't eat the shoots of the cannabis tree
Your mind shall spill unwound
And lie with the roots of the cannabis tree
Six feet underground.
Dance not with hell's fire;
Spurn ye virtue's thief:
Potación de guaya
Pot, the drink of grief

Years ago, debate was had;
We need not countermand it.
We banned the thing because it's bad,
It's bad because we banned it
And pestilential evidence
Shall die down, undermined.
We slept beneath the cannabis tree,
Its scent has sent us blind

LILAAAAAAC WINE
Is sweet and heady
LILAAAAAAC WINE
I FEEL UNSTEADY

Tide Pod Challenge

Do the Tide Pod Challenge
Swallow down your woes
Do the Tide Pod Challenge
They look like Haribos

Do the Tide Pod Challenge
Chug it for the win
Do the Tide Pod Challenge
Wash away your sin

Do the Tide Pod Challenge
Help Papa Darwin out
Do the Tide Pod Challenge
Prove yourself devout

Surely it's not challenging
To eat one little pod?
Brace before its cleansing sting
Open wide and nod

Treat it like a detox
Show them you're a man
Pick out a selection box
Send it to your nan

If the sweetie we provide
Revisits, re-emergent,
Try to stem the rising tide -
Then fail, and spew detergent.

Feel your throat grow swollen,
Stem your silent shout.
Irrigate your colon,
From the inside out.

Your mouth becomes a barman's tap,
Extruding foamy head.
Do the Tide Pod Challenge,
Then do being dead.

Idiocy knows no end;
Neither does compliance.
Do the Tide Pod Challenge, friend!
Do it! For science.

He I Mean She

he i mean she
is his i mean her
best advocate.
i meaning me
watch me watching him
i mean her
considering his
i mean her
identity. he
i mean her
providing my mind
(meaning the mind of i)
considerateness of his
i mean her
nomenclature.
i for myself would wish
him no offence no her -
none shall be done at a distance.
tunc dicturus, quid sum miser!
clad myself with sack and scissor -
thus i prepare with persistence.

i i mean me am antipronoun
me and my mind we do-si-do
stuck in an infinite hoedown
spinning impaled on a contrapoint
orbits ingressing a focus
slowly approaching the joint.

how to avoid distress at all?
through sins of omission,
silence. and through exactness
and literal repititition -
practise practise practise -
we get to carnegie hall.

Drunkard Song

A hopeless toasted sot am I
With little left to claw back
I get to drink and get to die?
Sir, tell me, what's the drawback?
So stick two kegs of Newkey Brown
Betwixt my little fists
And gaily shall I barrel down
The path that least resists
And should my lifespan sag and bend,
And should my face turn puce,
At least I just affect the end
That gets the lesser use.

Nuts

Nuts in a bowl
Crush the little suckers
Nuts in a bowl
Pulverise the fuckers
Watch them split in a vice-like grip
Hear that crack like a whip got whip
Socked with a punch that'll split your lip
Top of the nut split championship
The nut crack champ
Check my clamp
Rated number one in the nut crack camp
Pop that bubble, shell them hulls
I crack nuts like the cops crack skulls
Merciless wrath like badger culls
Swoop on the innards like hungry gulls
I gots the tools
They come exact
Get set fools 'cause you're gonna get cracked
Nuts on my street? Those nuts get jacked.
Step with my cracker and they gets attacked.
Nuts go snap like a sheet o'bubblewrap
Crack a sonic boom like a thunderclap
Too late nuts 'cause you're in my trap

That's all she wrote, like I popped a cap
I gots the moves
I gots the skills
I gots cashews
I gots brazils
Run run nuts head tward the hills
I'mma crack a nut 'til you get the chills
My vocation's nut devastion
Cracking up a nut like a cooked crustacean
Nuts get cut up
Can I crack a nut? Yup.
Buckle up buttercup,
Gonna crack yer nuts up
Bustin' nuts is real good, nut
Bustin' makes me feel good
You know what?
I think I'mma do it right now

KRAK

UH

...And Relax

Someone's got a klaxon
And warnings to emit.
This is not relaxing;
Quite the opposite.
Some fuckface and their sub-bass
Turned your guts to jelly;
It's very decibelly.
Your eardrum's wearing thin;
This gatecrash of a din
Is like a hefted welly
Against its tautened skin.
Tiring of their gabba,
You plugged your ears with wax,
And plunged your head in molten lead.
Now you're sexy sax
Overdubbed on Abba -
And relax.

You sweltered in Hell's Kitchen,
Half-asphyxiated
By burning belched-out bitumen.
Now you lie sedated.
Once you were spaghetti

Dropped in boiling pots
Until you found it petty;
You ironed out your knots.
Drained and baked and blistered,
The devil took the cracks.
The kids ran out of steam.
The kids ran out of scream.
You melted, then untwisted;
Now, relax.

Waking feels like war;
First you hear the yelling
Then rise to take a shelling
You did not sign up for,
And every time the mortars fell,
You legged it from the fight
And hid within your tortoiseshell -
Quite fucking right.
Living for conniption
And fibbing back at bluff
Is not your job description -
You are not paid enough.
So when you're in your dug-out,
Weathering attacks,
Go and nope the fuck out -
And relax.

Irritations gather
And flood up in a rush.
Try and take the blather
And turn it into hush.

Everyone gets ranty;
We, whom habit damns,
Like something out of Dante
Or Silence of the Lambs,
Must try and re-report it;
Flatten out the bends.
Watch our mind distort it
Like microbes through a lens.
Our preconceptions kept it
From tallying with facts;
We might as well accept it
Then relax.

Spontaneous Applause

Spontaneous applause
        for gays
Isn't really where it's at,
        these days.
They do not want my kind support
They bristle at my knowing wink.
They do not crave approving thought
They do not care what others think

Spontaneous applause
        for interracial couples
Engaging in mixed doubles
Isn't really where it's at
        these days.
        Rather like the gays,
                they'd rather go on,
                        unremarked.
Keep your condescending comments
        parked.

Whoops and claps
For trans people
        - as if they were, perhaps,

     Pan's People -
Isn't really where it's at.
They have sufficient troubles,
     like the gays,
Or interracial couples,
And need no ill-advised
Praise. It leaves them
Patronised.

Look how good I am, world!
Look how good!
By virtue of some single thing
I swagger, virtue-signalling.
Oftentimes, I don't, of course.
Show no gaudy outward signs;
     offer no applause.
Who would wish become some
Conundrum, a who-knows-what,
Curios, fripperies, like Ripley's
Believe-it-or-not?
Lord alive! Conumdrums
Displayed on a stage in cages, splayed,
Stuck in an age of aquariums?

Still,
Free to think, I need not care
That strangers labour unaware.
If they wish to know, then, know:
Should you feel rejected,
Persecuted, sidelined,
Ousted, maladapted,

Here you are respected,
Valued and accepted,
And, insofar as you so be,
Suchalike are we.

Gold Ferrari Outside Harrods

Your body is a mansion house
Its double doors your smiling mouth
Your holidays your jewelled watch
Your bank account your private touch
Expensive shoes your captioned friends
Your shining eyes your precious rocks
Your Instagram your fisheye lens
Your family your shares and stocks
Your devotees your kitchen staff,
Your laugh your French scent,
Your good intent, good credit,
Meditations, fiscal sense,
Enlightenment, fun.
Long white picket fence,
Payment for the labour done.
Assets and investment funds
Sold cheap by my comparisons.

Tell your tales. Philosophise.
Share it with us, if you must.
Sweetly-gently theorise
On how the world is love and trust
And, if, somehow, we don't believe it,

We may change how we perceive it.

What went wrong here? Nothing.
No flailing blame attached.
No-one died to give you stuff;
No capital mismatched.
No blue collars wound up screwed;
No drab vassals cry, eschewed.

Someone gets you. Someone gets
Full unhindered use of you.
Fate, the giggling fucker, lets
Someone get used to you.

As the admirable Hannibal Lecter said,
We covet what we see.
READ MARCUS AURELIUS, CLARICE
Of each thing, ask:
What is it, in and of itself?

Scary Halloween Costume

this year my
son jim wanted a
scary halloween costume so i
said jim why
not be a vampire he
said no i said jim why
not be a skeleton he said
no i said jim why not
be a zombie he said daddy i
really want to scare the
people we trick
or treat so i
said ok jim i
know just the
thing we dressed
him up in rags and
coated him in plaster
dust and made him
stare a thousand yards
away doused in fake
blood and jim said what
am i supposed to
be daddy i said you

are a little boy from
syria jim and trust
me it will put the
fear of living god in
our neighbours so we
went out at night and our
neighbours saw us and hurried their
own children
upstairs and hid
their sweets and fruit and
passports and locked
their doors and bolted
them and rang the
papers and immigration who
came and took jim
away so now i
have a costume too this
year i am a syrian
father who has lost
his little boy

The End Of The World, And, Therefore, The Book

It's The End Of *It's The End Of The World As We Know It And I Feel Fine* And I Feel Fine

As, ongoing, we plunge into the heart
Of the supermassive black hole,
Stipe, Buck and Mills emote,
Still without a permanent drummer.
Amid their final hit singularity,
In the spacetime of a rapid eye movement,
They spaghettify.
It's the end of
  "It's the end of the world as we know it, and I feel fine,"
   And I feel fine.

Stipe looks up,
Mournfully,
  his religion lost.
Buck,

though in the presence of a body that consumes all
electromagnetic radiation,
>is still wearing sunglasses.
Mills wonders which way is up,
Then follows Stipe's lead.
Truly, this time,
>Out of time.

*'Cause everybody huuur***WHOOOOOMP**

The End Of The World Is Always With You

When I was a little boy, my father sat me on his knee
And told me that death was the end, my flesh would rot,
The organs of my senses would putrefy
And so thereafter there would be no experience.
Well, I can take a lot on trust,
But who to trust?
I've seen things, man, I've seen things,
And I fancy I'll see a whole lot more before my time.

The celluloid runs quicker than the gaps between each frame.
You do not see the flicker, you only see the flame,
So what looks like projection to the unobservant glance
Is but a misdirection and the average of chance;
The end of the world is always with you.

Such things to which we might attest
Are beacons on the hills
Sequins sewn upon a vest
The winds amid the mills
The ridges milled around the coin
The tripping of the fuse
The dots our little children join

The crossword, not the clues.
We stake a claim upon a page and hustle death away
To ever live and never age; Tralfamadorian Grey.
But 99 point 9 percent of everything is nought,
And if a thing possess intent, perhaps it should not ought,
And if we seize point one percent then we have been mistaught,
For the end of the world is always with us.

We style our life an astral map;
We enter at one pole,
Then hurtle at the Southern Cross
To circumscribe the whole,
And what's the distance but a line
Marked up with felt-tip pen,
Continuously firm and fine,
To be traversed again?
From A to B to C to D to K to 5 to Omicron,
To i to pi to X to e, From Aleph Null to Aleph One,
To back to whence we had begun And thence to on and on and on,
A step's a step, but of what size?
Who marks our pace with golden rod?
And therein, thus, the problem lies,
For did we tread whereof we trod?
Our qualia are stepping stones upon an empty stream;
Faint intermittent chaperones who pass you down their beam,
And if that sounds as bare as bones, well, things be as they seem;
The end of the world is always with you.

Maybe life beyond the grave's like life before we were,
But birth beset our boats with waves and forced us to aver,
Marooning us in Plato's Caves, where all became a blur.

By stroboscopic light we slaves bethought we might infer
Such comfort and such smoothness as implicit in our sense,
Forgetting that it's useless for implying true events.
For no event is worth its note,
No lifetime lacks a lapse,
No fresco fronts the undercoat,
For God is in the gaps,
And the end of the world is always with you.

Notes

As I Was Saying Before I Was So Rudely Interrupted By My Own Indolence

Nothing much should be read into the mention of Xerox, the company which employed my father for the majority of his working life. No subtexts here, honest.

Be My Tory Wife

When performing this, I sound the final "F" phoneme by inhaling a "f-f-f-f-f-f", like Hannibal Lecter in Silence of the Lambs.

My sources tell me that the audience do not always initially twig that I don't like Tories, and the mood of the room warms as I progress through the poem.

Gove and his fellows used to do a weird thing with their thumbs, where you make a fist, poke a thumb out of the top and jab it to emphasise that you really really mean whatever bullshit point you're currently making. It's good that they've stopped this ridiculous habit, but it's not made them any more tolerable.

Betterer and Betterer

I keep notes on my phone of any ideas I have, and this is the result of trawling through the list and gluing it together. There's not really a grand design here, but I like how it turned out.

...cummings ist der dichter...

I don't know whether anyone else will like this, but I really really do. It's a sort of mashup of the thoughts and feelings I have around two pieces of music - Bach's St John Passion and Pierre Boulez's "...cummings ist der dichter...".

I love Boulez but this is not my favourite piece of his. I do, however, love the story behind its title. From "Boulez - Composer, Conductor, Enigma" by Joan Peyser:

"I was commissioned to write a piece for the festival at Ulm. I couldn't find a title for the work when they asked me what to print on the program. In a letter in German - my German was not very good at that time - I wrote: 'I have not chosen a title yet, but what I can tell you is this: Cummings is the poet.' A reply came from a German secretary who had misunderstood my letter: 'As for your new work, Cummings ist der Dichter....' I found that mistake so wonderful that I thought, well, then, that's a title given by the Gods"

Unrelatedly, "Jesus is coming, look busy" being tattooed on someone's arse is a plot point of the film "Johnny English".

Daliland

I wanted to address Dali's support of Franco and fascism, but didn't quite get round to it. Maybe later.

David Foster Wallace

I had wanted to write something about Wallace for a few months before I heard Setareh Ebrahimi was organising a Wallace night in Faversham. I was unable to attend, but I did at least finish this piece and share it with the other attendees via the internets.

The refrain is based, of course, on The Ballad of Davy Crockett, and the verses are a mixture of that "Plastic Jesus" song from "Cool Hand Luke", Tom Lehrer's "The Wild West is Where I Want To Be" and Linda Ronstadt's song about Mr Plow.

Jonathan Franzen is not "shit", but the internet is busily disliking him right now and it's fun to buy into that, unfair though it is.

Don't Stand So Close To Sting

For a long time I'd thought that the song ought to have gone something like "He liked to go and stroke off / To that book by Nabokov", but I realised I could be less crude, more to the point and more passive aggressive.

Re-reading the lyrics, I hope Sting isn't one of those awful people who thinks Humbert Humbert is a sympathetic character.

Dull Eyes

I once read a discussion online in which somebody posted a video of a new-agey chiropractor talking balls about how his subluxations could cure all your ills. The chiropractor was a young, pretty chap, with a very starey gaze. "Look at his dead eyes!", said the comments. Meanwhile, I meditate and notice how twitchy my eyes are, and how they calm down over time. Is this where I'm headed, then? Feels a bit like it.

Ebbsfleet Internal

"Ebbsfleet Int'l" is a sign I see on the A2 from time to time, and if you have read "Roster Gingham Chaam" in my last book then you will know I love a good abbreviated road sign. Anyhow, the idea that "Int'l" might mean something other than "International" was the initial idea that grew into this work.

I wrote some embarrassingly low-quality code to help me generate the word pairings in this poem and will share it if asked, but only with people with low coding standards.

Escalatorcleansers

For the Assemblance of Judicious Heretics, 2017 (see also "Heresy" and "Now He Is Both Sun And Moon"). The theme was "Revolution" and I hope I was not too oblique. Nigel Adams created a splendid visual piece to accompany it, which now hangs on my wall.

The inclusion of the Roman emperors is mainly due to my having read "I, CLAVDIVS" immediately before writing this.

"Chummy commie Candyman" should not be taken to mean that I think there is anything particularly wrong with Communism.

Escape Room

The Gravesend Panic Room is no longer on Berkeley Crescent, it's in the St George's Centre and is well worth a go.

Heresy

These works were written for the ventures of Medway publishers Wordsmithery. "Now He Is Both Sun and Moon" and "Escalatorcleanser" were written for their event "An Assemblance of Judicious Heretics", and "Memento Mori" and "Polestar Streetlight" were written for the excellent magazine "Confluence" (Issues 1 and 4 respectively).

I Do Not Particularly Care For Bands, See

This title is based on my previous work, "I Do Not Particularly Care For Banksy".

Is It OK To Punch A Nazi?

Obviously you need to base the answer to this question within some kind of context. I mean, it would be awful if someone went up to Richard Spencer in the street with no provocation and punched him in front of a filming camera which posted the footage online and it went viral. What?

"Yes, Virginia, yes" is a reference to "Yes Virginia, there is a Santa Claus", which Wikipedia tells me is the most reprinted editorial in the English language.

I Spell Well

Written for a dyslexia awareness event organised by the wonderful Sam Rapp.

It's Impossible To Learn To Plow By Reading Books

The title comes from a film by Richard Linklater, the director of such experimental films as "Waking Life", "Through A Scanner Darkly" and, um, "School of Rock". It's not what I'd call a good or enjoyable film, particularly when compared to the rest of his work, which is great. The title, however, was so ludicrous I had to try and do something with it.

The formatting's a bit odd, in order to try and communicate the weird meter needed to read it coherently. I should probably have set it as sheet music.

Kabaddi

In the sixth form, Channel 4 started broadcasting kabaddi and my friend Pali tried to teach us how to play it. To be honest, I'm not sure he really knew the rules. Anyhow, many years later (16?) I took my boy Jim to a kabaddi tournament at the Gravesend gurdwara. I still had no idea what was going on, but it was a fun day out. The Sikhs were handing out free curry, because they're awesome and that's what they do.

This poem, plus "This Poem Is Not About Gravesend" and "Escape Room", were written for an event at Woodville Halls, Gravesend organised by the artistic collective MUD.

Mary Berry

This is in no way supposed to represent the real actual behaviour of Mary Berry, who I am sure is lovely, not that I ever watch her on the telly if I can help it, not my bag.

Now He Is Both Sun And Moon

This was written for the 2016 "Assemblance of Judicious Heretics" event, organised by Wordsmithery. Poets were invited to write on a theme - in this case, the 450th anniversary of Shakespeare's birth - and artists were given the poems to write a work in response. You can, at current time of writing, still see Heather Haythornthwaite's excellent response to this poem on the Confluence website:

https://confluencemedway.wordpress.com/0220-now-he-is-both-sun-and-moon/

Nuts

This was written shortly before Christmas 2017, having bought a lovely new nutcracker for the festive season. When performing this, I whip out the nutcracker and a nut at the end, then crack it into the mic.

On the Eve of the Inauguration

Inspired by true-life events at Lisa Vigour's Inspirational Night at the Northern Seaman, Chatham. Some drunk took it into their heads that because of the imminent societal collapse that was to be Trump's inauguration, we had no right to be reading anything not relevant to that calamity.

The Pentagram Centre

For those of you not lucky enough to live in Medway, The Pentagon Centre is a shopping-centre-cum-office development built in Chatham in the 1970s. While its lower floors are a relatively well used shopping mall, its upper floors ("Mountbatten House") have been vacant for a very long time. Given the levels of homelessness in Medway, this seems criminally wasteful.

The Pentagon Centre does not have 15 storeys. "15 Storeys High" was an excellent sitcom starring Sean Lock and Benedict Wong.

People Dump

This poem is based on an actual place, which I won't name. But it's not in Medway and it's not Hartley/Longfield.

Polestar Streetlight

This one is about walking back from the station late at night. I don't mind the olde-worlde contrivances here, partly because I was inspired by the rhythms of Schubert's lied "Heidenröslein" (D.257). Having just looked it up on Wikipedia, mainly so that I could copy the umlaut, I see that there are lyrical similarities - there's a theme of plants and landscape in both. This is completely coincidental. 90% of Schubert settings are about plants and landscape and shit, they didn't have Nintendo back then.

Poor Leonard Cohen

I've never been a massive Leonard Cohen fan, and I don't know a lot about his personal life, but. Shortly after his death I read an article about how much of a ladies' man he was, but at the same time unable to commit emotionally to any of his partners or let them become sufficiently close to him. I don't know how true that is, really.

Richard Dawkins Eve

I have no great problem with Dawkins (or, as some online sceptic communities refer to him, "Dawkipoos") so this comes more from a place of mocking the idea that we atheists worship the most prominent among us as if they were saints or saviours.

Sleep Object

Written following a 19-hour fever-sleep, this is a pretty accurate description of what it felt like.

Tell Me The Truth About Art

I like the post-war Avant-Garde, but I get a bit antsy from around about Joseph Beuys (who I realise was a complex figure with many different aims, and plus I am pretty ignorant really). I will keep going to galleries and looking at things forever though, because it beats the hell out of football.

One room such as the ones mentioned at the end can be found in the permanent collection at MOMUK, Vienna.

"Clever chrome clone" is a nod to Blur's "Popscene" and their association with Goldsmiths and the YBAs, who I quite like but do not find transport me into rhapsodies.

The Awful People Show

"The Awful People Show" is the name my wife and I have for the popular light entertainment programme "Come Dine With Me", but I've appropriated it for my own purposes here.

The End Of The World Is Always With You

The title was inspired by Brad Warner, Zen teacher (he hates the phrase "Zen master") and punk bassist, who wrote a book called There Is No God and He is Always With You. I have not read this book, but it's probably worth a spin.

Tide Pod Challenge

This is a bit internetty, I'm afraid. Doing "The Tide Pod Challenge" consisted – and I use the past tense in the hope that people are not still doing it – of filming yourself eating a Tide brand dishwasher tab, something which, for health reasons, Tide do not recommend.

The "Do it!" at the end is to be read in the style of Shia LaBoeuf, i.e. look at someone as if you are very angry that they have made you carry a large, invisible beachball.

Vim Hymn

"Vim" is the program I am using right now to type this text. It is what old-school hardcore computer nerds use, and people who kid themselves that they fall into that category. If you imagine editing text on an old CRT screen with green text on a black background like they did in the 80s, that's quite possibly Vim being used. On the other hand, if I boot up a brand new Linux server tomorrow and I need to edit a file on it, Vim is a suitable tool for that job too.

Once one learns Vim one is quite probably its slave for life, but the actual process of entering text into Vim is non-trivial. Absolutely everything is supposed to be a time-saving shortcut, but remembering which time-saving shortcut one is supposed to be using is a hair-moulting stress. There are people at this very minute - this is a statistically provable fact - Googling "How do I exit Vim?".

This footnote is longer than the poem it relates to. As you will learn later in this book, I am a David Foster Wallace fan.

wat

"wat" is what people on the internet say when something is so nonsensical it doesn't even make no sense. I have used it as a catch-all for works that some might call "experimental". There's very little "experimental" about these pieces, I'm sure I'm retreading the ground of 50 years ago.

The material of this book was created using only free software: Ubuntu, Libreoffice, GIMP, Atril, Vim. Vim Vim Vim, Vimetty Vimetty Vim.

As with Book 1, I have sold out and taken the easy path by using Createspace, on the basis that it offered me a way to do a big brick of a book with minimal fuss. As I said in the introduction, I will hopefully now be purged of my ego and ready to co-operate with a proper publisher who pays their taxes, should one have me.

Front cover design: Me.

Thank you for reading.

https://zackdavies.wordpress.com

Also available:

Let The Big Fish Swim   (Zack Davies, 2016)
wrods   (Gerald Davies, 2015)

Printed in Poland
by Amazon Fulfillment
Poland Sp. z o.o., Wrocław